PROFESSIONAL DEVELOPMENT AND PRACTICE SERIES
ANN LIEBERMAN, *Editor*

Unions in Teachers' Professional Lives

Social, Intellectual, and Practical Concerns

Nina Bascia

Teachers College, Columbia University
New York and London

Published by Teachers College Press, 1234 Amsterdam Avenue
New York, NY 10027

Library of Congress Cataloging-in-Publication Data

Bascia, Nina.
    Unions in teachers' professional lives : social, intellectual, and
  practical concerns / Nina Bascia.
        p.   cm.
    Includes bibliographical references (p.) and index.
    ISBN 0-8077-3339-3. — ISBN 0-8077-3338-5 (pbk.)
    1. Teachers' unions—United States—Case studies.
LB2844.53.U6B37   1994
331.88'113711'00973—dc 20   93-45998

ISBN 0-8077-3339-3
ISBN 0-8077-3338-5 (pbk.)

Printed on acid-free paper

Manufactured in the United States of America

98 97 96 95 94   8 7 6 5 4 3 2 1

IN MEMORY OF

Bluma Vishnevetsky
Sam Kugler
Diana Weiss

Union activists in other places and times

From the Series Editor

The central task of the current reform movement in education is to build and transform schools that aspire to achieve democratic ideals. The purpose of the Professional Development and Practice Series is to contribute to this historic transformation by presenting a variety of descriptions of practice-oriented research-narratives, stories and case studies of innovative work that can lead to a deeper understanding of educational practice and how to improve it. At this time of important educational change we need to be informed by the special knowledge of university and school-based educators who, working in and with the schools, are illuminating how change can take place and what it looks like.

As new organizational arrangements and collaborative relationships are forged and studied, enduring organizational and pedagogical problems are being seen in fresh ways, leading us in new and promising directions. For example, even as the views of how teachers and students develop and learn change toward more actively engaging them in their own constructions of knowledge, the connections between teaching, learning, and assessment are being reexamined. The writers in this series, having undertaken to struggle with the problems of practice and the challenge of rethinking the future of the nation's schools, are seeking to involve us in this most important and ongoing process.

This book introduces us to another piece of the reform puzzle: the role of unions in treachers' professional lives. Although, in the last ten years, teachers' unions have played an ever increasing role in supporting—and sometimes constraining—school reform, little has been written about union strategies that support good teaching practice as well as higher pay and better working conditions. The popular image is of unions that work on bread and butter issues alone unconnected to teaching work. Nina Bascia has written an in-depth story of three schools, each representing different professional communities, where teachers' relationships and allegiances to the union are not the same. She analyzes the differences that local conditions make to teachers' commitments to the union and to the union's role, broadening or limiting teachers' conceptions of the relationship of the union to their professional lives. Her call for a new view of the connection between teachers' occupational needs and efforts to professionalize teaching helps us understand the potential for, in the words of Charles Kerchner and Julia Koppich, a "union of professionals"—a union that is sensitive to local context, to teachers' needs for support, and to the growing efforts to create schools that provide better learning conditions for both students and their teachers.

Contents

Acknowledgments

This study was conceived and conducted within the context of several active professional communities of scholars and practitioners, and benefited greatly from the support of colleagues and friends.

The Center for Research on the Context of Secondary School Teaching at Stanford University was my intellectual home between 1987 and 1991. The CRC funded much of the fieldwork and provided site access and numerous data sources. Colleagues' work provided important analytic overhead for my study: Leslie Siskin, Judith Warren Little, Milbrey McLaughlin, Joan Talbert, and Gary Lichtenstein's concurrent attempts to understand the various forms and dimensions of teachers' professional communities were of particular value. So were frequent, impromptu discussions with these colleagues and others, especially Hahn Cao, Marian Eaton, Stephen Fletcher, Jan Kerkhoven, Ann Locke Davidson, and Pat Phelan, on our emerging understandings of the lives of teachers and students in the schools we were all coming to know so well.

Milbrey McLaughlin's concern about the extent to which teachers' unions really move beyond traditional issues and strategies provided an important anchor for my study. Joan Talbert's interest in the collective action of other occupational groups and her competence and versatility with multiple forms of data rounded out the analysis substantially. Michael Kirst's broad perspective on educational politics encouraged me to develop careful links between activities at local, state, and national levels and to reconsider the distinctions between macro- and micro-level analyses. Jane Hannaway was a careful and thoughtful reader.

Teachers, administrators, and union leaders all gave generously of their time and expertise. This study would not have been possible without their belief in its importance and their concern that I get the story right.

Beverly Carter, Larry Cuban, Charles Kerchner, Julia Koppich, Ann Lieberman, Miles Myers, and Saul Rockman all provided research opportunities in school, district, and state-level settings that contributed useful examples of union sponsorship of educational reforms. Our mutual interests in educational improvement made conversations with these scholar-practitioners particularly valuable. I need to thank those friends, especially Diane Petropulos and Gary Tishkoff, who helped me keep my work in perspective by providing escapes from office and library. Finally, my deepest gratitude to Kathy Bickmore for ongoing support and inspiration.

Chapter 1

Teachers' Perspectives on Teacher Unionism

Teacher unions are major participants in American educational practice. As political interest groups, the American Federation of Teachers (AFT) and the National Education Association (NEA) lobby at national and state levels. As the legal representatives of teachers' occupational interests, unions have become more or less accepted players in school and district policy making. Over 60% of the country's districts are covered by formal collective bargaining agreements (McDonnell & Pascal, 1988): Union presence is a common feature of school organization. With 80% of the nation's teachers belonging to affiliates of the AFT or the NEA, union membership is an almost universal aspect of teachers' occupational identity. Despite the magnitude of these numbers, however, we know surprisingly little about the role unions play in teachers' professional lives.

American teachers have formed organizations around their occupational interests at many times and places, both in self-protection and to promote their own educational ideals. At the turn of the century, in the face of changing social and economic conditions and the emerging bureaucratization of urban education, many teachers, seeking to assert some degree of occupational self-control, joined what had been small, special-interest teacher organizations (Braun, 1972; Larson, 1977; Tyack & Hansot, 1982; Urban, 1982). Since the more recent unionization movement of the 1960s and 1970s, teachers have chosen collective bargaining wherever state laws permit it. Federal and state regulations have largely restricted the scope of collective bargaining to issues of teachers' wages, benefits, and working conditions (Carlson, 1992; Kerchner & Mitchell, 1986).

Teacher union issues have recently begun expanding in scope, however. Many teachers' organizations now publicly support and generate educational policy. Since the mid-1980s, the NEA and AFT have participated in educational reform discussions, and each national organization has developed its own ambitious strategies for school restructuring. At the local level, in a growing number of districts, unions work to enhance school and district capacity to support teaching and learning—securing new educational resources, creating structures for teachers' professional development, supporting teacher involvement in educational decision making, and considering a host of innovative services and programs that allow teachers to renegotiate their relationships with students, colleagues, and administrators (*American Educator*, 1987; Bascia, 1991; Casner-Lotto, 1988; David, 1989; Elmore, 1989; Johnson, 1988; Kerchner & Koppich, 1993; McDonnell & Pascal, 1988; Rosow & Zager, 1989).

Concerned with the status of teaching, some analysts contend that teachers' organizations should function more like professional organizations to provide occupational self-regulation and that they must work on improving public confidence in education (Darling-Hammond & Berry, 1988; Haberman, 1986; Kerchner & Koppich, 1993; Lieberman, 1988; McDonnell & Pascal, 1988; Olson, 1965). Other analysts believe that changing the substance of educational labor relations to issues more directly related to teaching and learning will result in more opportunities for teachers' participation in school and district life and will not only improve the quality of education for children but increase teachers' professional commitment and satisfaction.

For the most part, these arguments reflect the perspectives of union leaders, policy makers, and educational researchers. Whether the recent changes in union strategies effectively address teachers' occupational needs is another question. Proposals by administrators, policy makers, and scholars to "professionalize" teaching have often drawn teachers' citicisms for having failed to consider the realities of teachers' work or teachers' occupational values (Freedman, 1987; Haberman, 1986; Larson, 1977; Malloy, 1987; Matlock, 1987; Ozga & Lawn, 1981; Swanson, 1987; Sykes, 1986, 1987; Van Maanen & Barley, 1984). Contemporary teachers' understandings of the appropriate role for unions might well differ from those of these other groups. Despite the intention to increase teacher participation in educational decision making, the current discourse is largely void of any sense of what teachers might find useful or problematic about union representation, or indeed of any notion of the ways teachers value unionism in the context of their own practice.

This study considers the role of unions in teachers' professional lives, focusing on teachers' assessments of how unionism, in both its more traditional and newer forms, enables or constrains their work. It describes how teachers' evaluations of unions emerge from the context of local district and school histories, policies and practices, working conditions, and cultures.

SCHOLARLY PARADIGMS OF TEACHER UNIONISM

The mass district-by-district institutionalization of collective bargaining over the past 25 years precipitated several lines of research largely dominated by the pragmatic concerns of administrators and policy makers to learn to work around, and later with, these organizations. A recurring theme in the literature is that union presence focuses educational decision makers' attention on economic and political priorities, to the detriment of school programs (Kerchner & Mitchell, 1986; Louis, 1990; Mitchell & Kerchner, 1983; Simpkins, McCutcheon, & Alec, 1979). An influential line of scholarship has contended that collective bargaining promotes a conception of teaching as labor rather than as professional work (Carlson, 1992; Kerchner & Mitchell, 1986, 1988; Mitchell & Kerchner, 1983). This research blames union presence in schools and districts for encouraging the formalization of administrator–teacher relations and the standardization of teaching tasks (Englert, 1979; Johnson, 1984; McDonnell & Pascal, 1988; Mitchell & Kerchner, 1983; Simpkins, McCutcheon, & Alec, 1979; Williams, 1979). But teachers' voices are missing from these critiques. These assessments do not consider whether, or how well, collective bargaining addresses teachers' occupational interests or whether, in teachers' estimation, educational programs are improved or adversely affected by the collective bargaining process. Based on issues of concern to policy analysts, these studies do not consider whether or why teachers might value the regulation of their work.

Some of the earliest research on teacher unions looked for relationships among teachers' motives for union involvement during the organizing activities of the 1960s by studying correlations between level of union activity and teachers' personal characteristics such as age, gender, and ethnicity (Cole, 1968; Corwin, 1970; Lowe, 1965). This research emphasized the personal characteristics that teachers "bring to school," but it did not consider whether or how teachers' union commitment reflected their occupational concerns, or how unionism might be a logical response by teachers to particular working conditions.

Another line of scholarship has charted the general progress and substance of union issues and strategies (Englert, 1979; McDonnell, 1981; McDonnell & Pascal, 1988; Retsinas, 1982; Russo, 1979). This research has revealed that teachers' employment contracts tend to increase in scope, both becoming more detailed and covering a broader range of issues, as unions and school boards interact over time. But these studies focus solely on written contracts and on interviews with union officials and administrators, and they do not examine relationships between collective bargaining and teachers' real working conditions. Further, this research has little to say about the relationship between union gains and the quality of teachers' work lives. Contract provisions may reflect teachers' interests and experiences to some extent, but they also reflect the priorities of labor and district leaders who work at some distance from schools and classrooms. Understanding how well unions serve teachers' occupational concerns requires a different research focus.

One line of research on teacher response has more directly pursued the question of which union strategies are of most value to teachers. These studies, based on historical analyses and contemporary survey research, suggest that teachers typically have been skeptical and some-times even hostile when unions have moved away from "bread and butter" concerns to pursue teacher professionalism strategies or political agendas that encompass issues beyond educational matters (Densmore, 1987; Johnson, 1983, 1984; McDonnell, 1981; McDonnell & Pascal, 1988; Ozga & Lawn, 1981; Urban, 1982). Some scholars have concluded that teachers are "basically conservative" as a group (McDonnell & Pascal, 1988; Urban, 1982), while others have developed an evolutionary model to describe a "hierarchy" of teachers' needs, suggesting that economic security and basic working conditions must be ensured before teachers will turn their attention to other issues (Johnson, 1987; Kerchner & Mitchell, 1988). But these explanations are hypotheses. We need more contextualized analyses of teachers' occupational conditions and needs before we can accept these broader assertions wholesale.

In 1965, Mancur Olson published *The Logic of Collective Action*, contending that voluntary organizations such as unions have only a tenuous claim on member commitment. Unlike professional organizations, Olson argued, unions are not the sole providers of technical knowledge and have no legal requirement for membership. Because the goods and services unions provide are shared by large numbers of individuals, they are perceived as having inherently less value than goods of a more exclusive or elite nature. Olson believed that no "class consciousness" or "instinct" drives individuals to join groups and, because most unions are large organizations that operate at some distance from individuals' daily lives, members cannot interact within them in ways that are personally rewarding and cannot easily enjoy the fruits of their own labors or earn the recognition of their peers.

Empirical research on teaching and teacher unionism lends support to two aspects of the collective action theory. First, some studies suggest that teachers' commitment to union affiliation at the school, district, state, and national levels decreases as the organization becomes larger and more removed from their daily lives (Johnson, 1983, 1984; McDonnell & Pascal, 1988). Second, the assertion that the generic nature of union provisions may serve as a disincentive for membership commitment is consistent with recent research that describes the diversity of working conditions and variability of teachers' roles and professional needs (Johnson, 1990; Louis, 1990; Metz, 1990; Siskin, 1994; Stodolsky, 1988; Talbert, 1991). This research raises the question of whether a single organizational form can effectively address the range of teachers' professional needs—or whether unions can serve as meaningful sources of teachers' professional identity (see Lichtenstein, McLaughlin, & Knudsen, 1992).

Much of the research that tested the basic premises of *The Logic of Collective Action* found a strong and "illogical" tendency for individuals to contribute to collective action. Even in contrived experimental "game" situations where research subjects decided how much to contribute without ever meeting each other, it was not rational calculations but rather social considerations (how other subjects might feel or think, for example) that appeared to drive individuals' decision-making processes (Fleishman, 1988; Marwell & Ames, 1979, 1980, 1981; Marwell, Oliver, & Prahl, 1988; Oliver & Marwell, 1988; Smith, 1980; Sweeney, 1973; Van de Kragt, Dawes, & Orbell, 1988). Until now, however, researchers have not investigated the nature of members' commitment to real-world voluntary organizations, such as unions (Heckathorn, 1988; McCaleb & Wagner, 1985; Oliver, 1980; Yamagishi, 1984).

The collective action theory suggests two obvious research agendas, each representing a movement away from individual motivational issues to an emphasis on social and organizational concerns. One possible research strategy, focusing on unions themselves, would examine how these organizations structure opportunities for participation and set expectations for members' contributions. A second line of research concerns the relationships between voluntary organizations such as unions and the existing groups and structures they are intended to serve—for example, the roles of teacher unions within the social and practical contexts of teachers' lives in schools. Until now, educational research has not considered teacher unionism from either of these perspectives. Current attempts by teachers' unions to significantly enhance their roles in teachers' professional lives suggest that such research is of immediate and practical value.

UNIONS IN THE CONTEXT OF
TEACHERS' PROFESSIONAL COMMUNITIES

Recent research on teaching suggests that the value of unions for teachers is difficult to ascertain because of the complexity and diversity of what teachers do, how they think about what they do, and the contexts in which they work. Social and organizational differences in teachers' work may lead to substantively different instructional goals, practices, and professional standards (McLaughlin & Talbert, 1993). Teachers' work lives are shaped by administrative practices, time and material resources, the neighborhoods within which they work, and the students with whom they interact. Teachers' educational philosophies, subject area affiliations, programmatic specialties, and professional activities engender complex and varied conceptions of role, agendas, and identities (Bacharach & Mitchell, 1981; Clune, 1990; Johnson, 1990; Lichtenstein, McLaughlin, & Knudsen, 1992; Louis, 1990; Metz, 1990; Oakes, 1989; Siskin, 1994; Talbert, 1991). One way of making sense of this complexity is to consider the notion of teachers' "professional communities" and to explore how these communities interact with and are affected by teacher unions.

The term "occupational community" was coined by sociologists John Van Maanen and Stephen Barley (1984) to suggest that occupational groups identify themselves on the basis of their "collegial or communal" ties (p. 287) in ways quite different from the bureaucratic labels used by organizational theorists. Occupational communities are "group[s] of people who consider themselves to be engaged in the same sort of work; whose identity is drawn from the work; [and] who share with one another a set of values, norms and perspectives." (p. 287) Professional communities diverge in form and composition because they are "invented or discovered" (p. 295) by members on the basis of shared experiences and understandings. As used in this study, the notion of "professional community" elaborates the concept of "the same work" in two ways. First, it emphasizes that local organizational and normative features are important to community members' understandings of commonality. Teachers work in a variety of organizational environments that color, for example, the extent to which their work is understood as independent or collaborative, the extent to which they feel adequately supported, and the kinds of issues that draw them together with, or alienate them from, others. Salient aspects of teachers' professional community in one school might be quite different from those at another site.

Second, the notion of professional community explored in this study moves beyond a narrow conception of "work in common" to potentially include a commonality based on mutual support of the same broad endeavor. While some teachers might form relationships on the basis of particular categories of work—English teachers, for example, might find that their professional purposes and needs differ in important ways from those of math teachers—in some school contexts, teachers might recognize not only colleagues across disciplinary lines, but also administrators, school staff, parents, or students as contributing to the success and satisfaction of their own work.

Because professional communities are member-identified and locally constructed, they provide a more fruitful vantage point for the study of the value of unions to teachers than do the kinds of organizational analyses employed by many researchers. A number of union scholars have characterized teachers' interest in unionism as "selfish," assuming teachers perceive union benefits as enjoyed independently of colleagues and students and as divorced or distinct from work issues. The professional community perspective, on the other hand, explores potential links between teachers' work issues, including teachers' sense of loyalty to their professional community colleagues, and the value they find in unionism and work issues. Teachers' sources of support and struggle, their common issues, and the extent to which they see themselves engaged in a collectively shared or an independent endeavor vary, leading not only to different conceptions of who constitutes the "we" within the professional community and who the "they" outside of the community, but to different understandings of the union strategies that are most useful or constraining.

Across school and district settings, labor relations may be highly salient for teachers, or conversely teachers may perceive minimal effects on their work lives. In some contexts, teachers find that union strategies support their conceptions of good teaching, and union commitment provides a major source of their professional identity. In other sites, union activities appear entirely separate from, irrelevant to, or obstructive to teaching practice. By identifying, reinforcing, or responding to issues and values around which teachers find their common identity, teacher unions may contribute to the formation, composition, and boundary setting of professional communities. A union may speak for, or diverge from, particular teachers' understandings of their group identity.

In some settings, teachers' professional communities reflect formal organizational categories or hierarchical levels—academic department, school, or district, for example. In other locales, teachers' professional communities form around teachers' individual, idiosyncratic, less formally prescribed contact with others. In still other sites, teachers identify with others on the basis of a more general, abstract awareness of others' engagement in parallel enterprises across some distance. Teacher union strategies are likely to be more salient where they match the patterns and connections of a particular professional community.

The nature of teachers' interactions with others can be limited or fragmented, and teachers can make clear distinctions between their "purely social" relationships—the "casual camaraderie of the staff room ... at some distance from the classroom" (Little, 1990)—and their "purely professional" interactions—the kind of task-oriented relationships that occur within many academic departments and on school and district committees. In some work situations, teachers find opportunities to develop relationships based on complex blends of social, pragmatic, intellectual, and philosophical concerns. A union will have a greater shared value for teachers when it promotes issues that appeal to the most salient dimensions of teachers' community—where union activities that address work issues coincide with professional communities characterized by practically or logistically based relationships, or where union strategies of personal value, such as salary or benefits, meet relationships with strong personal dimensions. A teacher union may serve as a general locus for community membership where it encounters and interacts with community characteristics. Conversely, where union strategies do not match professional community issues, teachers may understand their union to be performing a valued but well-bounded function, or to miss the point entirely. The better the match between union strategies and professional community, the more likely a union will secure teacher commitment as well as enhance the practical and intellectual value of the professional community for its members.

THE STRUCTURE OF THIS BOOK

This study is primarily concerned with the strength and position of unions in relation to teachers' professional communities, and unions' roles in defining and promoting the workplace issues valued by teachers. The study contrasts teachers' work contexts in three high schools, each in a different district in California. Three case studies emphasize teachers' perspectives of the local union and other relevant issues during the 1988–89 and 1989–90 school years, a period when each local teachers' organization positioned itself to play a greater and more proactive role in district life. Despite this common phenomenon at the district level, the cases represent important school- and district-level differences in teachers' working conditions, different types of professional communities, and different perceptions of the value of unions.

Rancho (all names are pseudonymns) was a "strong union school" in Mostaza, a resource-poor urban district with a history of intense labor conflict. Rancho teachers' allegiance was with other district teachers across departmental and school boundaries; district administrators represented a powerful "other" because teachers perceived them as interfering with teachers' autonomy and their abilities to address students' educational needs.

Onyx Ridge was a relatively resource-rich school in an upper-middle-class neighborhood of Adobe Viejo, an urban district. Onyx Ridge teachers considered themselves independent agents and identified most strongly with subject area colleagues, who might work at schools elsewhere in the district and across the surrounding region. This diffuse notion of professional community, focused around curricular issues, was quite different from the one operative at Rancho. Onyx Ridge teachers were generally apathetic about the Teachers' Association.

Oak Valley was a large school in a wealthy, suburban district with a strong reputation for academic excellence and programmatic innovation. Here faculty were mixed in their opinions of the union, but teacher approval of the union had recently begun to increase. At Oak Valley High, teachers considered everyone who worked for the district to be part of their professional community, applauded reforms that enhanced working relations and garnered respect among teachers and administrators, and were suspicious of strategies that were seen to pit one group against another.

Chapter 2 describes the logic and strategies behind the construction of this study. Chapters 3 to 5 present the three case studies that illustrate how the particular contexts of school and district contributed to conceptions of teaching that evoked particular attitudes toward and uses for unions. Local events, values, and practices engender shared understandings among teachers with respect to the value of unions as potential sources of professional identification and vehicles for representation. Chapter 6 focuses on teachers' professional communities and the match or lack of congruence between teacher unions and other local organizational and normative features.

At Rancho, Onyx Ridge, and Oak Valley, teachers called upon their local union when they believed it was warranted by the particular conditions of their work. While the cases represent very different work contexts, Chapter 7 delineates how teachers across the schools, and even across levels of union commitment, had fairly consistent expectations of unions with respect to certain categories of union goods and services: Teachers expected unions to serve as a protection against excessive interference by others, to provide an option for representative participation in decision making, to secure instructional resources and personal economic benefits, and to ensure the recognition and respect of others for the realities of teaching.

Chapter 8 describes recent cooperative labor–management relationships, formal governance and representation mechanisms, and reforms intended to professionalize teaching at district and school levels. Contrasting the perspectives of union and district leaders with those emerging from teachers' school- and work-based contexts, this chapter recounts how these new arrangements had particular utility in relation to teachers' practical needs and particular forms of professional community.

Teacher unions can strengthen teachers' professional communities. They can extend their own organizational capacities to serve as sources of intellectual and moral inspiration for teachers. By paying attention to local professional community issues and values. Responsiveness to teachers' concerns should not be construed as a "narrowing" of the union role; the notion of a dichotomy between traditional collective bargaining and reform issues is not always productive. Instead, the case studies suggest that we reconceptualize the relationship between teachers' traditional occupational needs and efforts to professionalize teaching. Unions' successful involvement in educational policy and practice requires that the unions take seriously teachers' occupational needs as they are locally identified—for programs that improve teachers' practice, given their students, interests, and values, and their needs for support. Rather than assuming a generic organizational model, or a generic history of relations among teachers and others, unions must recognize and build upon the local professional community configurations that have best served teachers' professional, intellectual, practical, moral, and social needs. The case studies demonstrate the kinds of programs, structures, and services appropriate to different professional communities by describing instances of better and worse "matches" between local union attempts to professionalize teaching and the needs for support that teachers identify for themselves.

Chapter 2

Putting the Study Together

My interest in teacher unions emerged from my work as a graduate research assistant with the Center for Research on the Context of Secondary School Teaching (CRC), a federally funded educational research center housed at Stanford University, during the late 1980s and early 1990s. The CRC's mission was "to identify contextual factors and workplace conditions that influence how secondary school teachers think about and carry out their work" and "to analyze the policies and practices that enhance and constrain teaching and learning for different individuals in various settings" (CRC, 1989, p. 1)—to move beyond the sorts of traditional policy analyses that track single programs "down" the educational system, to "bottom up" examinations of teachers' experiences of the variety of social, organizational, and political features that constrain or enable their work (see Clune, 1990). As a founding member of the CRC research group, I participated in a working conference in early 1988, where selected educational scholars from across the United States helped to identify fruitful research strategies for exploring the complexity of secondary teachers' work. At this conference, the topic of teacher unions came up in conversation several times as a phenomenon that should not be overlooked, but, as the discussion made clear, none present could easily characterize these entities along any dimensions. It was the ambiguous or elusive nature of teacher unionism as a topic that first intrigued me.

During the same period, I followed the educational press in order to map out contemporary educational policy issues and to consider how teachers might experience this policy mix in the context of their work. Teacher unions were prominent in the educational news. There were increasing reports of the two national teachers' organizations' involvement in efforts to promote educational reform: The president of the National Education Association sat on the newly formed National Board for Professional Teaching standards, and the president of the American Federation of Teachers ran a weekly syndicated newspaper column on school restructuring. *Education Week* noted how local union leaders effectively advocated for teachers' increased involvement in decisions that affected their work—selecting principals, coordinating new programs, participating in development of new curricula, and establishing school-based decision-making structures. At the same time, reports of teachers' strikes in districts across the United States suggested that labor relations were a critical feature of many teachers' work. Both kinds of news stories supported the characterization of unions, at that first CRC conference, as having potentially powerful effects on teachers' work, but erratically so. It was becoming clear that different union strategies might have different effects not only on the formal organization of teachers' work but on teachers' identification with other teachers, with the greater educational organization, and with the unions themselves.

My perusal of the teacher union literature revealed that the research tended substantively toward issues of interest to administrators and policy makers and methodologically toward generalized depictions of union effects. It was difficult to infer how unions might be perceived by teachers and how these perceptions might vary across organizational settings. This missing teacher perspective became my focus.

SITE SELECTION AND DATA BASES

My affiliation with the CRC provided the opportunity to conduct fieldwork in and construct case studies around secondary teachers' workplaces. High schools represent particular settings for exploring the relationships between teachers' work and teacher unionism. As I and my CRC colleagues discovered, secondary schools provide a variety of possible configurations for teachers' construction of professional community. Teachers' subject area backgrounds and identities and the role of academic departments in organizing their work lives provide a greater variety of possible opportunities for within-school interaction than the less complex organizational structures of most elementary schools (Siskin, 1994; Siskin & Little, 1995). And, as we discovered by spending time in a number of different secondary schools, high school teachers' subject area affiliations also suggest a greater potential for external reference groups across school and district boundaries than what is available to most elementary teachers (see Lichtenstein, McLaughlin, & Knudsen, 1992).

I had access to schools in several different California school districts. This district-level variation allowed me to consider the salience of school *and* district-level features to the quality and nature of teachers' work, and to note unions' contributions to the structure of teachers' professional communities both within and outside of school. Districts are the determinant organizational level for a number of workplace features critical to the quality and nature of teachers' work: resource capacity, collective bargaining agreements, formal policies, administrative practices and personalities, the organization of time and space, teachers' participation in decision making, and opportunities for collegial interaction.

During the 1988–89 and 1989–90 school years, CRC colleagues and I conducted "core" interviews and observations that focused on teachers' conceptions of teaching and perceptions of students, the various roles and functions of academic departments, and collegial interactions among teachers. I spent between 60 and 80 hours in the three schools used in my research, and several days with district-level personnel. I also spent between 10 and 20 hours at each of two other high schools in Adobe Viejo and two other high schools in Mostaza. This fieldwork helped me distinguish between those features of teachers' work that could be attributed to district-level characteristics and those unique to particular schools.

"Snapshot" research has its limitations: Time plays as critical a role as location in fixing and delimiting organizational studies. As the case studies demonstrate, history provides a powerful lens through which teachers interpret new events, but the cases also suggest that meaning changes over time and over the course of events. Shifts in policies and practices at any level, changes in student and community characteristics, differences in faculty composition, alterations in administrative and union leadership all may lead to changes in the meaning and value of unionism for teachers. Even during the brief period of this study, teachers' attitudes toward their union underwent discernible shifts. The construction and resilience of the value of unions for teachers would be enhanced by revisiting the same schools over a longer period of time.

I initially designed my study as a comparison of high school teachers in two districts, Adobe Viejo and Oak Valley, that were engaged in cooperative labor relations with those in a third, Mostaza, still characterized by traditional, and highly contentious, labor issues. But events do not stand still and wait for observation: The school year during which I conducted my most intensive fieldwork, 1989–90, began with the establishment of new cooperative labor dynamics in Mostaza; as a result, the study contrasts three cases of "new unionism," albeit with importantly different histories and results.

I selected schools within these three districts on the basis of "core" interview data. Two general rules governed the selection process. Because the collective action literature led me to consider the importance of organizational features such as size and structure in relation to teachers' commitment to voluntary organizations such as unions, I wanted to study schools that differed along those dimensions. At the same time, I felt it was important to limit the number of structural differences among the cases. Second, choosing to focus on the array of union issues relevant to teachers at the district level, I ruled out schools where teachers were clearly dissatisfied with building administration. I also ruled out schools with special missions, such as magnet schools, reasoning that such schools can displace teachers' sense of collective interest with teachers in other schools and thus affect union attitudes and role in the school context. Rancho, the "strong union school," intrigued me from the beginning. I decided to contrast its nontraditional cross-disciplinary and participatory management structure with a relatively traditionally organized school, Onyx Ridge, and a highly departmentalized school, Oak Valley. I believed I had selected schools where teachers relationship with site administration were not particularly contentious, but teachers' concerns about administrators in two of the schools—Rancho and Oak Valley—turned out to be relevant to teachers' expectations for union representation.

INTERVIEWS

A list of individuals quoted in the text of this study—both union respondents and others from different interview sets—is provided in the Appendix. I contacted the most senior union representative at each school, described my study, and asked her or him to characterize the major roles and issues of the teachers' organization in the school. I also asked this person to "map" the faculty in terms of level and expression of union commitment. School union representatives, like the district-level union officials I also interviewed, were enthusiastic about the study and offered me various kinds of support. They had copies of documents made for me and invited me to observe meetings. One school representative offered to recommend me for honorary union membership.

With the senior union representative's help, I identified a number of potential respondents, more than I expected to actually interview, in order to compensate for any logistical complications or teachers who might be unwilling to talk with me. I identified teachers who represented a range of attitudes and levels of commitment toward the local union—teachers highly favorable, who currently or previously served as union representatives; teachers who were union members but, by their own admission, were minimally committed or ambivalent about the value of union strategies; and teachers who were not union members and were strongly opposed to the local union in particular or to unionism in general. I also wanted the full sample to reflect a range of academic departments and different lengths of tenure in the school and district. In some cases this meant approaching a teacher who had not been interviewed previously by anyone in the CRC, but in other cases it meant returning to a teacher who had been interviewed before.

Nearly all the teachers I interviewed seemed reasonably comfortable with the topics of our conversations and were willing to be tape recorded. The few cases of obvious discomfort included a senior representative's request that I turn the tape off while he spoke "off the record" in order to protect the reputation of a principal; a teacher who revealed that his participation in various job actions was precipitated by pressure from school colleagues; and a respondent concerned about expressing his feelings because of his level of anger with union leadership. Despite political risk and charged emotions, however, these respondents spoke frankly.

I found teachers generally appreciative of the opportunity to express their concerns, grateful for what they found to be insightful conversations, and hopeful that their perspectives might contribute to a greater understanding of the realities of teaching. Over the course of the study, a number of teachers and administrators approached me whenever they saw me in the halls, wanting to tell me the latest developments. Nearly every respondent, from those most involved in union activities to those "on the other side"—even those with little initial understanding of my interests—was concerned that I "get the story right." Their concern about an ignorant public seemed to outweigh any fears of political reprisal. Several took pains to explain the logic of the other side to me.

Because I was interested in understanding teachers' reasoning, interviews were deliberately open-ended rather than tightly structured around protocol questions. In this way, respondents could suggest appropriate analytic categories and relationships, and emerging themes could be pursued during the course of an interview. To make sure it was consonant with her or his intent, I made sure to articulate my understanding of the respondent's words as the interview unfolded, a strategy that often prompted further reflection and discussion. The following topics were covered over the course of each conversation through a natural progression of issues and in response to probes:

The respondent's professional history, particularly in the school and district; teaching assignment and extra-classroom roles; closest colleagues; and the nature of working relationships.

The respondent's level of involvement with the union; and the particular issues, events, or values that the respondent believed were relevant to that level of union commitment.

The respondent's perception of union commitment across the school; and the particular issues, events, or values that the respondent believed led to various levels of teacher commitment.

The respondent's perception of union organization, issues, and strategies, in both historical and contemporary terms.

I conducted similar interviews with teachers who could provide historical perspective on union activities, school and district administrators, and district-level union leaders. Asking these individuals to "map" and explain teachers' attitudes toward, and involvement with, the local union helped locate respondents within the broader teacher population and provided historical and contextual background to teachers' perspectives. Because I was interested in the construction of meaning, I understood all the teachers I interviewed, whether knowledgeable about union activities or not, as both informants and respondents—that is, both as union "experts" and as representatives of their own idiosyncratic points of view.

I was sensitive to teachers' busy schedules and tried to arrange to meet with them when they felt they could spare some time during a prep period or after school. Interviews extended anywhere from 20 minutes to 2 hours, depending on teachers' time constraints and interest in the issues, with the average lasting about 45 or 50 minutes. While some teachers appreciated the significance of my study, others did not—unionism held uneven salience for teachers. While I had concerns that some teachers would be uncomfortable discussing such a potentially politically volatile topic, of the 26 teachers I contacted, only three refused to participate.

Over the course of my fieldwork, I pursued several tangential themes. I wondered whether and how academic departments might serve as loci for particular union attitudes and selected more than one teacher from those departments that had reputations for housing a number of union activists. After a teacher identified a close colleague as the impetus for her own union involvement, I interviewed several "best colleague" duos to see what could be learned about the sharing of perceptions and values. At Oak Valley, I included teachers involved in the Faculty Advisory Council and the Oak Valley Colloquium, once it became clear that these bodies served union-like functions.

I was fortunate to be involved in an evaluation project that brought me into contact with a dozen local union organizations attempting to establish collaborative relationships with district administrators. My research on educational policy trust agreements (Bascia, 1991; Lieberman & Bascia, 1990) allowed me to understand the nature of the gap between the perspectives of district-level players and teachers' experience of district and union policy.

I obtained and read monthly bulletins and newsletters sent to teachers, minutes from union meetings, teachers' employment contracts, and documents pertaining to union-sponsored programs, such as written cooperative agreements, training documents, and workshop materials. I collected school documents such as student and faculty newsletters as well as news clippings about the school and district from local newspapers.

DATA ANALYSIS

Each school site was different in terms of the apparent density and complexity of union issues in school affairs. The consistency of teachers' responses varied from school to school, as did the ease and certainty with which I could infer relationships between teachers' attitudes and what I knew about other social and organizational features.

Data analysis followed a version of the process described by Glaser and Strauss (1967) as the "constant comparative method," an iterative process between theoretical considerations and encounters with the data. Careful readings of the union interviews and other interviews conducted in these schools by myself and other CRC researchers led to the development of themes, which were further developed by returning to the literature and discussing the issues with colleagues. The development of the concept of "professional community" emerged out of these collective understandings (see also Little & McLaughlin, 1993; Siskin, 1994; and Siskin & Little, 1995 for other treatments of this theme, including some analyses conducted in these same schools). For each interview, I wrote an analytic summary using an emerging descriptive and analytic coding system. In all, I analyzed 33 supplementary interviews for the Onyx Ridge case, 27 for Rancho, and 46 for Oak Valley. I then constructed the three school cases and wrote the cross-case analyses, working out my conceptualization of teachers' professional communities.

Because of this study's short time frame and the diversity among the school cases, it was not truly possible, or appropriate, to conduct analyses of possible causal relationships among particular structural, attitudinal, and demographic features of the schools and teachers' attitudes toward local unions. For example, while the Rancho case suggests—

and respondents in other districts have concurred—that academic departments can be the locus for forming attitudes toward and uses for the local union, departments did not consistently serve this function, and teachers within a department did not necessarily report consistent levels of approval or disapproval for union strategies. While certain historical events held strong salience for some teachers, it is not the case that teachers present in a district at a particular time always reflected consistent responses to those events.

Instead, it was my intent to develop *plausible inferences* about the social construction of teacher unions in the context of teachers' work lives. While earlier union research tried to identify the causal factors that contributed to teachers' support of unions, often at the individual level of analysis, I assumed that the importance of unions to teachers was embedded in workplace conditions and professional community characteristics—that the value of union presence and membership must be understood in the context of teachers' collective experience and understandings. I drew upon observations in the schools and teachers' expressed understandings of issues and events. I noted the persistence or variation among those understandings and looked for plausible explanations as reflected in site data.

No case study-based research can explore all the influences on, or dimensions of, teachers' work: The selection of case study rather than survey research entails a trade-off between depth and breadth. This study is intended not to develop a comprehensive typology of teachers' professional communities, but rather to suggest some of the diversity of teachers' working conditions and professional needs. The study demonstrates how different local teachers' professional communities are, and how profoundly different teachers' needs for union protection, representation, and professional interaction can be. If anything, the constancy across the cases in terms of state policy context, the comprehensive nature of the high schools, and the fact that the case districts were all engaged in establishing cooperative labor relations underscores these points. Studies of other secondary schools with more diverse organizational structures and missions, of elementary schools, and of schools in other districts and states would reveal somewhat different professional community configurations and issues. The implication is that unions must be sensitive to these differences if they are interested in engaging teachers not only as union members but as active participants in school and district life.

Chapter 3

Rancho High School

There is this little island called Rancho.

                    —A social studies teacher

Strife, stress, chaos.—An English teacher

Once things got to a certain point, even if they offered you a solid gold coin it was going to be hard because people at that point would want two gold coins.

                    —Senior Teachers' Association representative

RANCHO AND ITS TEACHERS

In 1975, Mostaza Unified School District established a new high school and invited district teachers to apply to teach there. Of those chosen, many had participated in the development of innovative educational projects at other sites. The new staff—self-consciously "extremely capable," "leaders, opinion setters," "risk-takers"—was given free reign to develop curriculum and services around their perceptions of student needs and interests. In the early years, Rancho's teachers traversed the country, observing student-centered programs in action and culling the most attractive ideas for consideration by their own faculty. They established cross-departmental "learning houses," early versions of schools-within-schools, to provide a "sense of community" and encourage personal relationships among students and adults. Teachers and administrators served as "advocates" for students, maintaining these relationships for the duration of students' tenure at the school. Rancho's school governance structure involved faculty, staff, students, and parents and entailed "leadership training, training in conflict resolution, shared decision making. It was a very innovative school; it was going to try and set a brand-new trend in education. As a teacher, I could have input over what happened in the school," recalled an art teacher. Ac-

cording to a former principal, "Rancho was ahead of its time. It embod-
ied what all the [more recent] commission reports recommend."

Many teachers were involved in professional activities outside the
classroom: They "served on district committees, and we have fought the
good battle at the state level and the National Council of Social Sciences
and things like that." Along with what some characterized as "academic
activism" came a particularly strong identification with the Mostaza
Teachers' Association. Rancho was a "strong union school" in a strong
union district. Teachers' commitment to the Teachers' Association dated
from the school's inception when, as some of the original staff members recalled, some of the staffing decisions were based on deliberate
attempts to defuse some of the strong union sentiment in another district high school. It is impossible to account for teachers' professional
community at Rancho High without considering the union's central role.

Rancho teachers recognized "a direct and positive correlation between strong Association and other leadership positions across the board.
Maybe activists are activists are activists." For at least some teachers,
union membership contributed to a feeling of entitlement to participate in decisions about a host of work-related issues; in an interesting
pattern of overlapping leadership, a number of department chairs, learning house leaders, resource coordinators, and chairs of the school governance council served consecutively or concurrently as union representatives. Teachers' Association issues and the Association's authority
were considered routinely in the course of school decision making. A
comprehensive collective agreement and teachers' working knowledge
of its provisions led to a belief in the legitimacy of union involvement
in a variety of situations—teaching assignments, evaluation, scheduling,
and student discipline—where administrative decisions affected teachers' work. According to the union representative of longest standing,

> [At Rancho, department heads and other teacher leaders] are
> fairly strong people. They make sure that things are running
> along according to contract, and when things are not going the
> right way I will get a little note, "We really need you to come
> into this meeting because we think we're being sold a bill of
> goods." They're smart enough to realize that there may be a vio-
> lation or a potential violation down the line, so sometimes I can
> say, "OK, these are the guidelines." I'll bring them a copy, and
> they'll go in and they'll solve it before I have to get officially in-
> volved. In other words they'll tell the administration, "We really
> don't want to see the staff divided." And our administration has
> been reasonably good that way.

Nearly all of Rancho's classrooms and offices were contained in one large, single-story building, and because of teachers' habit of congregating in public spaces, it was relatively easy for union representatives to test the faculty mood on an informal basis. According to the senior union representative, "Sometimes what happens is I'm down in the lunchroom and they're talking and they don't even realize but they're venting some of their frustrations, and sometimes I start to see a pattern in their frustrations." This teacher took particular pride in his sensitivity to faculty concerns and to the prompt administrative attention that nearly always resulted from his intervention.

> It's been small kinds of things, [for example] a couple of classes overloaded and the administrators don't clean it up as fast as they should, and so we rattle the cage with the complaint process, and most of the time those get solved. It's been probably 8 years since we've had really hard-line grievances that have gone downtown. Most of the time the minute we go in and discuss it the problem gets solved.

In 1989, 13 years after its opening, Rancho had the largest student body of any secondary school in the district, with approximately 1,700 students, and was still the newest. It enjoyed a positive reputation among other district teachers "because it's large, it has lots of facilities for teachers, more chances to try something different or new, it's aesthetically pleasing." "There's a certain amount of jealousy because we're a relatively new school," an art teacher believed. "The staff here is more viable than at other schools in the district." Rancho teachers' successful entrepreneurial efforts to acquire instructional resources resulted in "a lot of extra money to spend," and close working relationships with support staff afforded teachers "a lot of secretarial help that other schools don't have. We have a lot of benefits the other schools don't."

Rancho's founding structure and identity retained an important place in teachers' conception of their school. Teachers' cross-departmental collegial relationships endured, fostered by the complex governance structure and Rancho's own blend of social, curricular, political, and student-oriented discourse. Teachers continued to rely on their multifaceted relationships with colleagues to advocate for students. An industrial arts teacher, for example, described how if "we have a mutual student whom we have a problem with, we'll get together and discuss it, say what we can do to get the kid working." In exchange for repairs on other teachers' cars and classroom equipment, he expected to be able to ask for a "return of the favor": "If I have a problem with a student who's in sports, I can go out to the coach and say, 'Hey, this kid really needs some leaning on, let's lean on him.'"

On closer scrutiny, however, by 1989 much of what distinguished Rancho from other secondary schools seemed to have eroded. Table 3.1 identifies some of the major events that seem to have shaped and re-shaped Rancho teachers' workplace context. Some of these changes were the inevitable results of shifts in staffing. Teachers still met weekly with their advisees in a sort of homeroom, but when the school lost its coun-selors in the early 1980s as a result of a shortfall in district funding, the advisory system lost much of its strength. With two substantial influxes of teachers, once in 1981 when ninth-grade teachers were moved to the high schools, and again in 1986 when the district initiated a magnet school plan, the faculty's commitment to "the Rancho plan" suffered, since a significant portion of the new teachers were "leaving somewhere else" and were less than completely enthusiastic about the features that made Rancho unique.

Changes in the school were also the result of the difficulty of sus-taining cross-disciplinary instructional programs (see Siskin, 1994). Where Rancho's learning houses once experimented with innovative scheduling and courses, over the years instruction became increasingly conventional. In part this was a response to new state and district cur-riculum policies, but innovation also suffered because of the time de-mands of teachers' daily teaching loads and the difficulty of "designing a curriculum around the particular talents of 22 individuals who hap-pened to teach in the same learning house."

District policies also had their effects on the school. In the late 1970s, with changes in the superintendency and school board, the climate that had fostered the establishment of a school like Rancho no longer existed; instead, the newer district initiatives emphasized standardization and centralized control of curriculum and evaluation and a closer supervi-sion of principals. In 1989, considering these changes, what rankled teachers the most were the district's attempts to manage features of their work that teachers believed they themselves were best qualified to con-trol, such as the selection of textbooks and other instructional resources, and control over staff development. The district's new directives affected not only teachers' individual curricular choices but the collective au-tonomy of the faculty. Prior to centralization efforts, according to an art teacher, "you had staff input, shared decision making, you felt like you had control of your fate. When they centralized they took away the control of the school; they made edicts outside the school, you felt to-tally helpless." Rancho's governance council lost its authority as the school's decision-making body as the principal became the sole authority recognized by district administration "and he had to take responsibility for our decisions, and he started overriding decisions that the school governance council made or not using the council as a vehicle." Teachers believed that their principal protected them from the district's most egregious attempts to interfere in their work, and their sympathy for the difficulty of his position kept them from directly challenging the erosion of staff decision making.

Finally, the school changed as a result of a decline in teachers' feelings of competence in response to changes in the student population. In 1985, a court-ordered desegregation plan changed Rancho from a predominantly white and middle-class school to a diverse mix of classes and ethnicities. The number of non-English-proficient and low-English-proficient students increased substantially. Many students commuted to school from the other end of the district. "I remember when we couldn't even find a poor family to give a food basket to at Christmas," said an English teacher. "We had other problems, but we didn't have the problems that poverty brings. Now we do in spades." Teachers found it hard to deal successfully with students who were less motivated to come to school. A second English teacher:

> Education is not [the first] priority [for the new students]. . . .
> The court [desegregation] monitor should ride the bus every day for one solid month to see what it's really like for these kids, and to be subjected to the different gang aspects on the bus and to the insults and the inconvenience. . . . The draw is where your friend is going, where your boyfriend is going. You'd have to have a pretty secure kid to say, "Gee, I'll call you tonight and we'll talk for an hour and I'll tell you what I did in school today." These kids don't have that kind of self-assurance, their self-esteem is low, and they want to be with their friends, they don't want to be separated.

Students transferred in and out of the school throughout the year, making it more difficult for teachers to manage the sequencing of course material or to get to know the students as individuals. Many were clearly frustrated by their inability to interact with students in any of the ways that had worked for them in the past. "Giving students an opportunity to see me for some extra help after school," for example, an effective means of working with students who lived in the neighborhood near Rancho, was not an option for students who spent several hours a day crossing the district on a bus (see Phelan, Davidson, & Cao, forthcoming).

TABLE 3.1 Salient events, Rancho High School

YEAR	UNION	DISTRICT	SCHOOL
1971		First desegregation suit filed	
1975			Group of faculty help design building and plan educational program
1976	Collective bargaining law passed in California		School opens
1977/8	Collective bargaining election in Mostaza district; administrators leave Teachers' Association; first contract		
1979		State Proposition 13: 17 schools closed	Loss of school counselors
1981	End of caucus structure; beginning of presidential and executive director structure. 11-day strike with 92% teacher support	New superintendent. 38,000 students. Loss of 575 teachers between 1980–83	1,500 students. Teachers file 37 grievances
1982	3-year contract signed with substantial pay increase for teachers	Bankruptcy filed	New principal. Change from 3- to 4-year high school; influx of junior high teachers and 9th grade students
1983/4		Desegregation trial. Senate Bill 813 (state omnibus education bill) brings new money to district	
1984		New superintendent, new school board, increased centralization	2,100 students

TABLE 3.1 *(continued)*

YEAR	UNION	DISTRICT	SCHOOL
1984/5	3-year contract; small salary increase	Court desegregation order	Influx of teachers when another district high school is closed
1986		New superintendent. Desegregation plan goes into effect. Beginning of magnet school plan. 38 schools; 29,500 students; 1,350 teachers	1,800 students including lottery-selected students from across the district (desegregation plan)
1988/9	"Work to rule" order	Teachers stage wildcat sick-out; students stage sympathy walk-out; 225 students leave district as a result of labor conflict	"Work to rule"
1989/90	Contract settlement; Contract Oversight Group; cooperative labor relations; win-win negotiations training. 90+% union membership	New superintendent. 41 schools; 1,550 teachers	All new administrators including principal; 75 teachers; 1,650 students. 96% union membership

Despite the enduring rhetoric about its student-centered orientation, it was difficult to mobilize Rancho's faculty around the new students' needs and interests. Some teachers looked to the district for training and guidance and were frustrated by the lack of response. Others believed the solution lay in additional school support staff and teachers with particular areas of expertise, and accused the district of mismanaging staffing; still others felt that too many teachers were close enough to retirement not to have the necessary willingness and energy to learn new ways of working with students. In 1989, teachers' lack of satisfaction with their interactions with students was deeply debilitating.

LABOR RELATIONS

Labor relations had been a prominent feature in Mostaza district teachers' work lives for more than 10 years. Prior to 1977, when collective bargaining was initiated, the Mostaza Teachers' Association (MTA) was the "professional organization" to which nearly all teachers and administrators belonged; "in the years [before collective bargaining] we held teas," recalled the MTA president. The first legally binding collective agreement, according to the union president, "had an awful lot of professional language in it, [for example] we had language that all district committees were comprised of a majority of teachers." Collective bargaining changed all the district rules and regulations concerning teachers' roles and responsibilities that had been negotiated earlier and changed all the nonbinding "may's" to more emphatic "will's." "Our relationship in the district essentially changed. Our bargaining unit had had administrators in it, and now we had administrators out of it." It was difficult for "the old boy network downtown" to adjust to the formalities of a legal negotiating relationship. Before collective bargaining, resource allocation was a matter of trust: A district administrator might find funding to fulfill a teacher's request "[even though] you didn't see those few dollars on any line-item budget, or they'd say, 'You can't do anything because there's no money there.'"

The move toward district centralization of authority during the last few years of the 1970s further eroded the trust level between union and administration. In 1980, when the union asked for a substantial raise for teachers, the district refused to comply. The Teachers' Association hired an executive director with a record for organizing successful strikes, and teachers struck for more than 2 weeks. In the end the district conceded to Teachers' Association demands, teachers went back to work, and the district filed for bankruptcy. The Teachers' Association president understood the move as "a deliberate attempt to destroy our contract." Ten years later, district administrators were ready to concur with union leadership that the district had acted in poor faith.

Through successive superintendencies and a variety of fiscal circumstances, Mostaza teachers saw their salaries decline relative to those of other teachers in the county, and teachers' salaries persisted as the major labor issue. Between 1980 and 1990 there were three impasses in contract negotiations as the union made a series of attempts to increase teachers' salaries and the district chose "financial conservatism" even at times when, according to a former district administrator, "we probably had the money to add another percentage point and probably should have."

The Teachers' Association campaigned actively to keep teachers' distrust of the district alive, but teachers' "bad feelings left over from the first strike" were reinforced by a pattern of the district "saying there was no money and then finding x number of millions of dollars at strange times," "spending thousands and thousands of dollars on maintenance, on things that were ridiculous." Teachers found it "very difficult to be objective about, because if you read the newspaper, read the district's own balance sheet at the end of the year, [you see that] they lie to us frequently, they admit it frequently."

At Rancho, the salary issue was salient in and of itself, but teachers also saw parallels between the district's refusal to agree to salary increases and a more general lack of support for teaching in general. The social studies department chair:

> It's being treated like a child all the time. Like we're not doing our job. Even when you do your job the strokes aren't there. . . . [Mostaza is] an urban district that has never recognized the fact that it's grown. It's like a huge farm district. We have farmers on the school board who don't acknowledge the urban problems.

"How much contact do we have with the district office?" asked another department chair. "As little as possible! They send us requests." According to the senior union representative, "It's very rare that you see anybody from downtown administration out on the building site unless the whole thing is just ready to blow sky high. And then they come out wearing a different hat."

A YEAR OF LIVING DANGEROUSLY

In 1988, the union prepared to sign a new collective agreement that included the school district's offer for a moderate salary increase for teachers. As the time for signing the agreement approached, however, union leaders "began to realize that, wait a minute, there is more money there, we understand that there's more money there." To the Teachers' Association, and to teachers, the district appeared once again to have been less than honest about available funds. Put to the vote, over 95% of the teachers rejected the district's compromise salary offer. In district newsletters and the local papers, the union criticized the district's spending patterns and its practice of keeping money in reserve—tactics that seem to have aroused public sympathy for teachers but also, teachers later felt, diminished their professional reputation in the community. The existing collective bargaining agreement expired and for over a year it was not clear how the stalemate between union and district could be resolved.

When their contract ran out, most of Rancho's teachers began "working to rule"—only performing duties specified in the last collective agreement. The school governance council, learning houses, and academic departments all stopped meeting formally. According to the art department chair, "Some departments shut down and some [did] not. Our department [met] because we're all friends, we usually eat lunch together." Teachers were less willing than ever to participate in the advisory system, even after the principal warned them that, by refusing to meet with advisees, they were "shooting themselves in the foot." Plans for new projects initiated by teachers and other staff during the previous year—a peer observation program and staff development geared toward effective teaching strategies for the new student population—came to a standstill. A department chair was aware that, without meetings "you lose the big picture, the sense of the whole," but many teachers felt that "we just aren't going to kill ourselves when we don't feel that there is any payoff there." According to the senior union representative, "Once the staff feels they're being railroaded, they're gonna throw sand and rocks and all kinds of things into the gear system."

Teachers' morale plummeted. A physical education teacher new to the district was sensitive to "a lot of grouching, a lot. There's one table you don't even sit at at lunchtime anymore, but by accident I did and then I said, 'Why did I do this?' It was just negative, negative, just spewing out." Some teachers' comments suggested that the demoralization reached into the classroom. As a social studies teacher perceived it, "[The superintendent's lack of] concern or respect for the teachers shows up in class. Teachers say they are not working as hard, they pretend to be working, they're unhappy, their hearts are not in their work."

Many teachers were angry enough to want a strike. The Association president found that his most difficult task

> . . . wasn't moving the conservative campuses to a point of being ready to [strike]; it was to keep the other extreme, which had been ready to strike since September, from coming apart . . . to keep the real militant schools from self-destructing and running off in some other way or doing some wild-cat things that would end up having us splinter.

The president identified Rancho as "one of the most militant schools," but then went on to name over a dozen other schools where nearly 100% of the faculty stayed away during a "sick-out" that teachers organized without the Association's official sanction. Teachers held informational meetings openly during lunch. According to a vice principal, "I'd have to be blind not to know when people were meeting and who was meeting." Rancho teachers did their own picketing as well as organizing activities at other schools. According to an industrial arts teacher, "We've done a lot of things that [teachers at other schools] have not, like leafleting and picketing the airport when the mayor has dignitaries there. Those kinds of things were our ideas."

Rancho teachers experienced a see-saw: "'We're on strike—we're not on strike,' and that just created a tremendous amount of stress that was very unsettling." A teacher described that school year as "going about my business, attending meetings, picketing. During the picketing I passed out doughnuts." Some teachers struggled with the notion of striking, and social pressure clearly played a role in their decisions, but many believed they ultimately had no choice. A teacher who said he "[picketed] because I didn't want to deal with the hassles [from colleagues] if I didn't" also claimed he "[didn't] trust [the district]" and believed that "the only reason we were [working to rule] was that if we didn't do it, you're really in a situation where nobody was going to come out winners." For one of the few teachers unsympathetic with the union, it was "constant turmoil, awful paranoia. . . . I didn't like it because the kids say things like 'Well, are you going to go out on strike?'" For district administration, the level of tension made that year "worse than a strike."

Late in the spring of 1989, the superintendent resigned and was replaced by a former deputy. The new superintendent initiated a series of summer negotiation sessions that ended, literally hours before the first day of the new school year, in a tentative agreement. Teachers received a moderate salary increase, some long-contested safety and resource issues were resolved, and district and Association leadership pledged publicly to maintain a more cooperative working relationship. A "Contract Oversight Group" was established to continue working on contractual issues throughout the year: "A lot of the nickel-and-dime irritant issues can go to them instead of having 700 items on the bargaining table." In a potent symbolic gesture, the district and Teachers' Association brought together principals and union representatives from each school so they could hear "the same explanation" of the contract and then present it to their faculties. District and Teachers' Association leadership, their respective bargaining teams, and the Mostaza school board embarked on a series of training sessions in consensus decision making and conflict resolution throughout the 1990–91 school year.

Rancho's principal and senior union representative saw some of this new spirit reflected in teacher–administrator relations at the school. What had always been a cooperative relationship between principal and senior union representative now had the formal approval of district leadership. This year, according to the current principal, "when we talk about concerns, we're saying 'we.' 'We need to address this,' or 'Let me share with you some things people are saying,' and 'What can we do?' and 'Let's work it out together.'"

Rancho's principal believed some of the tension was alleviated, but "that wasn't the end. The strike was settled and we came back to work, but it wasn't over. Because things continue to happen. A lot of people feel fine right now, but some people don't." A relatively new teacher saw that "people are beaten down. Look at the age of the faculty and think about what they've been through: desegregation, bankruptcy, going from one of the highest to one of the lowest salaries in the county." While teachers no longer officially worked to rule, Rancho's governance structure was not up to full steam and new extra-classroom projects had not yet begun. "No one's had the energy to get them going again after last year. The district doesn't know how much ground was lost when they put us through this. It's hard to break the habit of working to rule. All those little intangibles. . . ."

While teachers valued the role the Teachers' Association had played in securing improvements in their salaries and benefits, many teachers were less certain that the shift in labor relations made any important difference in their work lives. While the new collective agreement included some small concessions in instructional resources, most teachers did not experience increases in their resource levels. There were plenty of indications that the district's support for teaching had not appreciably improved, and teachers saw the features that had been the school's strengths in the past continue to be undermined by district actions and inactions. While the Contract Oversight Group endorsed in principle the notion of site-based shared decision making, the district was "going slow," encouraging a faculty governance plan at only one district school and only on an experimental basis. Despite the faculty's expressed wishes that their interim principal be made permanent, a new principal was selected for Rancho High from outside the district. In fact, all of Rancho's administrators were transferred to other district schools and replaced by new staff unfamiliar with the Rancho plan and unable or unwilling to support the school's innovative programs. Increasing numbers of non-English-speaking students continued to be assigned to the school.

When teachers discovered they would be paid only minimal wages for special summer planning sessions to work on the superintendent's plan for converting Rancho to a magnet school, the majority voted against supporting the plan. Few teachers were willing to assume positions of school leadership. House and council structures remained under-utilized, and teachers reported that their working relationships with colleagues were still strained. With union issues ostensibly resolved, conditions were far from satisfactory and teachers had lost their traditional vehicle for active resistance.

An English teacher framed these changes as a natural result of school evolution.

> You know how schools have peaks and valleys? I think this school reached kind of a pinnacle about 2 years ago and it's starting to go downhill. Because the teachers are old and the original intent of Rancho has kind of run its course. [One of the new administrators who had been at the school in its early days] is talking, she's using the same language and she has the same philosophy as the original Rancho, and it's like an anachronism. People just don't want to hear it, they don't want to do it. They just want to be left alone.

However well this assessment captures the role that teachers' professional career stages fill in school climate and programs (Huberman, 1991), it misses the significant role that the teachers' organization played, and might play, in Rancho teachers' sense of occupational satisfaction.

TEACHERS' PROFESSIONAL COMMUNITY AND THE TEACHERS' ASSOCIATION

Rancho teachers identified strongly with other teachers regardless of specialization and the size of their professional community was district-wide. Like many other districts at this time, Mostaza's teacher population was primarily older; teachers of long tenure had taught together in other schools before Rancho and shared a common history. They considered district labor history a crucial part of new teachers' socialization: An English teacher told how "last year when we had the [walkout], as younger teachers came in, they were quite starry-eyed and we old veterans sat down and explained this long history of things to them." The district's tendency to recruit administrators from outside the district rather than promoting teachers from within served to intensify teachers' feelings of alienation from administrators and identification with the teaching force. In Mostaza, if they stayed in the school system, teachers would always be only teachers.

At the school level, Rancho's architecture and history of cross-specialization relationships afforded teachers the perception that they shared a common purpose. Teachers' collegial connections were multifaceted. According to an industrial arts teacher, "They're working relationships, they're social relationships during the day as well as after school hours. So it takes in all spectrums of it." Even as the faculty became increasingly demoralized and socially disconnected, this history of access to colleagues' social and work lives encouraged teachers' awareness of their colleagues' personal and occupational needs. Because the Teachers' Association's value to the professional community was understood to promote both individual and collective, personal and occupational benefits, even a nonunion member was sensitive to how

> . . . teachers get desperate. I think . . . to be raising a family, to have a wife who may not work, to want to educate those children and send them to college, and realize that [a neighboring district] will pay $7,000 more a year than Mostaza, you become angry.

Because of this understanding, although she was unwilling to participate in Teachers' Association actions herself, she found herself "torn between being able to do what I want to do versus doing what's good for the collective whole."

Most Mostaza teachers felt they *were* the union or, more precisely, that union strategies flowed, or should flow, from their own occupational needs. Teachers perceived parallels between the district's bad faith relationship with the union and the erosion of district support and resources for teaching: the losses of school counselors, release time for leadership positions such as department chairs, opportunities for professional development, and classroom materials. The union's strength within teachers' professional community derived from the strength of teachers' own convictions. In some instances, the Teachers' Association directed teachers to active protest, but at other times, when they felt the Teachers' Association was not moving quickly enough, teachers took matters into their own hands. The intensity of feelings led to divisions among teachers, but even in this atmosphere of "strife, stress, and chaos," it was difficult to disentangle teachers' commitment to the Teachers' Association from their commitment to each other: Even those uncomfortable with the notion of striking struggled with whether they could really let their colleagues down. An English teacher described how

> People were too angry to suit me. The [union] meetings would upset me and so I would choose not to attend them. And then I

began feeling guilty about that. [My colleagues assumed] that if you're not at the meeting you're not committed and you don't care, and that wasn't necessarily true at all. I think some people felt, "You just don't care enough about us, you're not one of us. You are separating yourself." . . . It was a real moral dilemma for me.

Rancho teachers, in sum, strongly identified with other teachers irrespective of subject background or school location, and as educational activists accustomed to making curricular and programmatic decisions. The district's direct challenges to their authority and autonomy caused them to perceive administrators as "they" rather than "we." Teachers' long-standing affiliation with the Teachers' Association was reinforced by the parallels they perceived between the district's neglect of their own requests for support and its bad faith relationship with the union. As the Teachers' Association became less clearly supportive of teachers' identified needs, however, it lost its position as the touchstone of teachers' collective identity. The loss for teachers was both practical and emotional. Teachers felt they no longer had recourse to their last remaining option for effective representation, and as a result their overall commitment to teaching suffered.

Chapter 4

Onyx Ridge High School: Professional Teachers Make Up Their Own Minds

We're not close-knit, but we're professional.
                                —Social studies department chair

The union is just something that I belong to, but I'm not involved with it really. . . . It's there and it's nice to know that
it's there in terms of teachers and their needs and concerns.
                                —A foreign language teacher

Teachers probably wouldn't do things very differently if the
Association weren't here.—A social studies teacher

ONYX RIDGE AND ITS TEACHERS

Onyx Ridge High School was built in 1981 in an upper-middle-class
section of Adobe Viejo, a quickly expanding city, in response to parents'
rigorous campaigning for a high school in their own neighborhood.
Onyx Ridge students' test scores were among the highest in the district;
nearly a quarter of the 1,200 students qualified for the gifted program.
Parents showed strong support for school programs and often volunteered to support teachers' efforts; even working mothers would "come
in on their off days to help proctor an exam, that kind of thing, they're
here in a flash." The administration was "supportive—they haven't for-
gotten what it's like to be in the classroom." Teachers understood Onyx
Ridge as "probably the number one place to be in city schools," "utopia," "there's no better place to go. Teachers say they want to retire from
here."
Onyx Ridge teachers had been "hand picked" from other district
schools and saw themselves and their colleagues as the "creme de la

creme" of the Adobe Viejo district, "lots of superstars." Staff selection was still controlled through the principal's masterful manipulation of district hiring and transfer policies. Onyx Ridge students felt entitled to express their likes and dislikes, but teachers' competence was taken for granted; staff understood that student complaints reflected "personality [conflicts], not a matter of whether a teacher is good or bad. There are no bad teachers."

At the beginning of each school year, Onyx Ridge's principal asked all teachers to volunteer for at least one of the school-wide committees that covered a range of curricular, extracurricular, student service, and social topics. Teachers were also encouraged to expand their professional roles through a variety of activities in the greater educational community in the region. Onyx Ridge teachers characterized these variously as "professional duties, simply one of the things you accept, just as you accept so many other things that go along with being a professional"; or, more positively, as "expansion, allowing me to stay as a teacher but still [opening] a lot of other doors." What these divergent comments have in common is the extent to which such activities were considered an important aspect of Onyx Ridge teachers' professional identities.

The faculty were "here for the students." They worked hard on their classroom performance. An English teacher's sense of professionalism encompassed

> . . . coming in prepared and working past the allocated hours to get things done, and meeting with students and meeting with their parents, and it seems in order for every day to go more smoothly there are things that have to be done which probably are outside of the job description or what you would hope the hours would be.

A strong norm of individuality operated at Onyx Ridge. Once a teacher arrived, he or she was expected to perform well as an independent agent. Teachers could approach designated "mentor teachers" for instructional ideas or assistance, for example, or plan lessons with other teachers, but these collegial interactions occurred at teachers' own initiative and teachers spoke about them in terms that suggested the privacy of the exchanges. Neither professional norms nor policy or architecture supported routine collaborative work. The school boasted the largest number of designated "mentor teachers" of any secondary school in the district, but at Onyx Ridge these positions were understood as "recognition that there are teachers who [are already doing] exemplary work." Some teachers attributed the absence of collaboration to the school's physical layout: Only science teachers could claim a departmental workroom, and the two staff lounges were too small for staff to meet in any sizeable number. Teachers said they were too busy working on their classes to seek out collegial interaction. A chemistry teacher denied feeling isolated and unsupported. "Oh, no. The bottom line is [a teacher's] competence and the core idea of being willing to help kids." Another teacher believed that "the pressure comes from ourselves. I think that everybody wants to be a good teacher. We set high standards for ourselves." Teachers' in-school interactions seemed distant; they knew of each other primarily by reputation.

The sparseness of salient events itemized in Table 4.1 attests to the remarkable extent to which Onyx Ridge teachers seemed oblivious to issues and events occurring outside their own independent professional circles. In a district grappling with the social and educational needs of an increasingly diverse student population, Onyx Ridge was something of an anomaly. By mandate of a court-ordered desegregation plan, nearly one-third of Onyx Ridge's students were actually transported to the school from a low income, mixed ethnicity neighborhood across Adobe Viejo. Yet Onyx Ridge teachers' attention was focused primarily on the students from the neighborhood surrounding the school. Teachers acknowledged that students participating in the desegregation program tended to be academically and socially isolated from neighborhood kids, and some teachers were aware that the black and Latino students could easily "fall through the cracks." But teachers' largely self-directed style of work contributed to a general belief that individual teacher incentive, and not school-wide programs, was the appropriate means to address student needs; there were few avenues, formal or informally sanctioned, by which teachers could advocate for students about whom they were concerned.

THE TEACHERS' ASSOCIATION IS NOT MY BAG

In 1990, labor relations were not as prominent in teachers' minds as they had been in earlier years. Adobe Viejo schools reflected a 60% Teachers' Association membership rate district-wide, with some schools claiming over 90% membership. Onyx Ridge's membership stood at around 50%—like that at Rancho, this was by design, according to some teachers, who believed that initial staff selections for the school were made partly on the basis of teachers' lack of interest in the Adobe Viejo Teachers' Association (AVTA). The teacher union president attributed Onyx Ridge's low membership rate to teachers' identification with the upper-

TABLE 4.1 Salient events, Onyx Ridge High School

YEAR	UNION	DISTRICT	SCHOOL
1976	Collective bargaining law passed in California		
1977	Teacher strike		
1981			Some teachers hired to "get school ready"
1982		New superintendent	School opens
1986		First district plans for school restructuring	New principal
1987		First restructuring implementation	
1988/9	3-year contract with superintendent's involvement; "mutual respect;" Contract Oversight Group established.	School board adopts "core curriculum" plan; 166 schools. 2,450 teachers; 70% union membership district-wide	1,240 students; 54 teachers; 50% union membership

middle-class status of the neighborhood—"they think they don't need the union." Teachers in 1990 were working under a 4-year collective agreement.

A strike 10 years earlier and the subsequent annual work slowdowns around contract resolution remained memorable events in teachers' minds. The principal recalled rounds of "voluntary picketing from 7 to 7:20 in the morning and then, because school started at 7:25, [the teachers would] all sign in at 7:25." The teacher who assisted the Teachers' Association representative with union activities in the school described how "in September we'd come back to school and wouldn't have a contract. So then we'd start a little job action, withholding services." Teachers did not recall these actions as particularly effective: Despite their yearly efforts, the Teachers' Association did not achieve what teachers would have considered significant salary increases or sufficient improvements in working conditions. Even a teacher who supported the union could understand her colleagues' irritation.

We'd go through all these strategies and they would bring in the
impasse team from the state and it just got frustrating, it seemed
like the same old same old. Nothing seemed to help. I think
there were people who were frustrated and said, "Hey, AVTA is not
doing anything." And when all these job actions didn't work,
some people just dropped out [of involvement with the union].
Because [the union] just wasn't doing enough.

A nonmember's conversations with other teachers left her with the
impression that

That was our one major strike, 8 or 10 years ago, and people still
talk about it, "Oh yeah, I was pulled out on that strike," and
they're still not happy about it. "I lost all that money and I got
back in and I don't feel like that much was handled." So I think
now they'd have an even harder time getting people to strike because of what they did last time.

While some nonunion members believed the Teachers' Association
wasn't militant enough, others "would like the Association to just butt
out and let the district do what they will." Some teachers contended that
the AVTA lacked a record of successes sufficient to inspire teachers' commitment. A social studies teacher stated:

The union is almost like a political party: There are so many concerns and needs among its constituents that it's difficult. In order
to be all things to all people, which is pretty much I would say
the direction the AVTA has taken, that tends to weaken the full impact of what it might accomplish.

Whether supportive of the union or not, Onyx Ridge teachers were
unified in their priorities: The Teachers' Association should focus on
decreasing class size and substantially raising teachers' salaries. In the
absence of productive activity in these areas, many teachers found the
union largely irrelevant to the quality of their work lives. Teachers who
generally supported the AVTA saw its value as lying elsewhere: "They are
an organization where people can take individual grievances, that's very
important. I think probably as much as anything, that's where their
strength lies."

But at Onyx Ridge, the security the AVTA promised lacked a critical
edge: The union was "there almost as a back-up" because teachers found
their work relatively free of the kinds of obstacles they would consider

calling on the Association to rectify. Onyx Ridge teachers responded much more favorably about the quality of their working conditions overall than teachers at Rancho. "Why would you need Association protection for your job unless you have hassles?" asked a teacher who did not belong to the Teachers' Association. "And there are so few things that you can be hassled about in teaching. Why would you think of the Association if you don't need that support and you never use it?" In Onyx Ridge teachers' experience, critical educational issues were handled by parties other than the AVTA: "The other things that I'd like to have taken care of, in terms of maybe low achievers or high achievers, I think parents take care of all those special interests. Someone does, maybe the federal government does. But I feel that most of those ideas, concepts, are taken care of." Finally, representation issues were handled at the school level in ways that teachers felt sufficed. Site administrators were supportive and receptive to teachers' needs. Teachers' involvement in school decision making took the form of a "principal's cabinet" of department chairs that not only determined how school resources were allocated but was a productive means of alerting the administration about potential problems. A union member commented:

> I think if teachers feel they have a forum for complaints or concerns then they're less inclined to feel they need a strong union. The administration here is very willing to run interference for us. And I don't think they do that consciously saying, "Oh goody, this will keep them from going to the AVTA." I think it's seen as, "This is a genuine concern, someone needs to do something about it," and they're willing to pick up the ball and run with it.

In some schools, like Rancho, union representatives serve as liaisons between teachers and site administration, but Onyx Ridge teachers were likely to approach administrators directly rather than involve the site representative. The site representative in 1989 was a former district-level union officer whose image as an activist during the Teachers' Association's formative years, and the fact that he was not one of the school's original "hand-selected" group, created a distance between him and some of the faculty. This teacher volunteered to serve as union representative only when no other teacher stepped forward; at Onyx Ridge "it's always hard to find teachers willing to serve as site rep." The union representative's activities in the school consisted of inviting teachers to stay after general faculty meetings for any issues they wished to raise and ensuring that teachers received information that came from the Teachers' Association. Onyx Ridge teachers appreciated his "low-key" approach.

What teachers seemed to find most salient about the AVTA was its call, during earlier rounds of annual contract disputes, for teachers to limit their extracurricular work—a request that seemed out of context in a district without contractual language concerning the amount of time teachers should allocate to various duties, and a request that many teachers understood to be in direct conflict with their professional values. A social studies teacher, not an Association member, remembered when "the people that were in the union were really riding the people not to do any extra supervising, not to write letters for kids, and these sort of things that hurt the reason we're here." Even the alternate union representative conceded that

> Anyone who is a teacher, who is an effective teacher, there's no way that you can get things done in 40 hours a week, you take things home. So with the rule of really encouraging people to work only your 40 hours, what do you do? You don't do your clubs anymore, you don't write recommendations, not because you don't want to but because those are things that are over and above what you need to do to run your classroom, to teach your kids. In some situations that was really hard on the kids, and that was hard for a lot of us.

Some teachers were angry at the AVTA for "issuing orders" that constrained their own sense of professional judgment. A social studies teacher recalled how "a few people in the PE department were asked by some not to do this or that and it got into a shouting match in the lunchroom because the athletic director said, 'Don't you even begin to tell me what I should and shouldn't do.'"

Teachers' comments suggest that whether their colleagues were Association members or not held little social relevance at Onyx Ridge. According to one nonmember, "They're very low key here. There are those that are strongly supportive but at least they're not harassing you." Teachers could not identify strong pro- or anti-Association cliques or departments within the school; at Onyx Ridge "your friends don't necessarily have to agree with you." Teachers seemed to independently determine whether joining the Association, or being an active union member, suited their individual styles, circumstances, and values. A foreign language teacher said:

> If I was into the real philosophical issues, yeah, I would probably join. . . . I think that one needs to belong just for protection, but I really can't say I would become a union activist, although I can

see that sometimes we need to stick together. [Who gets involved in the Association?] Probably the kind of person who's going to get involved in any cause, and if they feel really strongly about certain issues I would think they'd want to get involved. . . . An activist: Some people are, some people aren't.

Teachers who chose not to join the Association framed union membership as in the same way any other professional commitment. According to one teacher, "I don't feel that I could always comply to what they wanted us to do, and I couldn't feel that I was a member worthy of what they think being a member should be." Another teacher said that "if I were ever to join I'd be very active and outspoken about it. That's the way I am about anything I get involved in." At the same time, there was no strong correlation between Association membership and teachers' willingness to support Association actions and issues: Some nonmembers picketed before school in recent years, while a relatively inactive Association member chose not to because, as she said, "I don't see myself as carrying a sign." Even teachers adamant in their dislike for the Association expressed a willingness to support Association actions if and when class size or large salary increases became serious bargaining issues. "There are times that even though I'm not a member and they were asking for support in certain things that I thought were important, I would feel like I would be able to contribute."

THE SCHOOL, THE DISTRICT, THE ASSOCIATION, THE FUTURE

In the late 1980s and early 1990s, many schools across the Adobe Viejo district attempted a variety of new projects and programs. The district instituted a "core curriculum," subject by subject, intended to eliminate ability-level tracking and provide a consistently high quality of instruction for all students. Many sites began year-round programs to alleviate school overcrowding, dividing students and staff into smaller schools-within-schools that permitted more personal relationships among students and staff. Some schools experimented with cross- and interdisciplinary teaching. The district established a professional practice school in collaboration with a local university. Many of these reforms had already been initiated when the district and Teachers' Association signed a 4-year collective agreement in 1988; once the contract was signed, the Teachers' Association actively began to support the district's restructuring plans, adding its endorsement to existing projects and collaborating with the district on a new peer coaching program for teachers. The Teachers' Association and district formed a Contract Oversight Group, much like Mostaza's, to discuss contractual issues in nonadversarial terms on a monthly basis. The combination of new district programs and cooperative labor relations enhanced teachers' and Association officials' participation in many district-wide decision-making bodies.

"If It Ain't Broke, Don't Fix It"

The union's new prominence at the district level did little to increase its profile at Onyx Ridge. Even with the AVTA's endorsement on district communiques to the schools, few teachers seemed aware of the extent of, or the reasoning behind, the Association's involvement in district policy making. With their attention focused primarily on the middle-class, neighborhood students who composed the greater part of the student body, the faculty generally were uninterested in considering the new options, such as peer coaching, for their school. When forced to respond to district mandates for changes in curriculum or school structure, teachers typically reacted negatively. The elimination of ability-level tracking was seen as an infringement on teachers' professional judgment and as inappropriate for Onyx Ridge students. "You are going to have a lot of bored students and you are going to have a lot of students where it's way over their heads and they are going to be really struggling and the teacher is not going to have the time to help them," warned a math teacher. Encouraged by a joint district–Teachers' Association committee to consider a shared decision-making structure, Onyx Ridge's principal's cabinet of department chairs quickly decided that the staff had as much decision-making authority as it needed: In the principal's words, "If it ain't broke, don't fix it."

There was less incentive than before to serve as union representative. With the 4-year contract, there was less urgency around bargaining issues; the new contract had dispensed with the few "perks" union representatives had enjoyed in the past; and because the Contract Oversight Group assumed decision-making authority over issues that previously would have been taken up by the greater Teachers' Association, the Representative Council meetings were now "blah. There are no good issues."

Onyx Ridge was coming under increasing pressure to respond to district restructuring plans, and it seemed likely that the role of union representative and the visibility and importance of the Teachers' Association would shift, but whether they would be enhanced, or whether the pressure to adopt these changes would drive teachers to a stronger opposition to district policy and union strategies, was not yet clear.

TEACHERS' PROFESSIONAL COMMUNITY AND THE TEACHERS' ASSOCIATION

Onyx Ridge teachers described their faculty as a loose coalition of autonomous agents. Culled individually from a number of other district sites to teach at this special school, teachers, despite their long tenure in the district, seemed to lack any of the sense of historical commonality that was such an important aspect of Rancho teachers' professional identity. They perceived themselves and their colleagues as different from other faculties by virtue of their expertise, their students as different from other students by virtue of their academic achievements, and their school as different from other schools by virtue of the quality of their working conditions. At the same time, the school was not the most salient boundary in Onyx Ridge teachers' descriptions of their professional communities: Many Onyx Ridge teachers expressed their greatest satisfaction in their involvement in subject area–related activities that stretched not only across the district but throughout the entire local region. That a social studies teacher was considering a possible career move to a nearby suburban district exemplifies this sense of transcendence of traditional organizational boundaries. Occupational boundaries also were mutable: Onyx Ridge teachers discussed moves into administration in the same way they might consider a new teaching assignment, as options for individuals to "do something different." The opportunity to consider such options made Onyx Ridge teachers less likely than Rancho teachers to adopt an "us and them" perspective with respect to administrators.

The school's physical organization afforded teachers few opportunities for collegial interaction: There were no places for teachers to work together or even to socialize. Teachers made a distinction between their "professional" interactions and other kinds of relationships. A math teacher, for example, identified her closest school colleagues as two other math teachers, but at the same time stated, "I don't socialize with teachers in my personal life. . . . I prefer not talking business when I'm not at school." These distinctions, coupled with Onyx Ridge's culture of individualism and the sense that professional teachers "aren't in it for the money," meant that, unlike at Rancho, Onyx Ridge teachers did not link personal economic and professional issues or consider Teachers' Association issues in terms of their social or collective value.

Teachers found their professional autonomy relatively unhampered by district policies. Until recently few curricular mandates had come down from the district level, and teachers could rely on the availability of instructional resources and support staff. School administrators were seen as particularly effective in shielding the faculty from "interference" from downtown. With few links between the Teachers' Association and teachers' workplace issues, teachers' union commitment was further minimized.

Onyx Ridge teachers' commitment to the Teachers' Association was consistent with their sense of themselves as professionals. Decisions about joining the Teachers' Association or participating in Association-sponsored actions were made on the basis of teachers' independent experiences, values, and calculations of the importance of supporting an agent whose primary "good" was a protection against hypothetical inequities targeted at individual teachers—a service of little practical or moral value. Increases in district pressures on the school might give teachers something in common to rally around. In that case, because of its support for district programs, the Teachers' Association would likely be perceived as being "on the other side."

Chapter 5

Oak Valley High School: The Significance of Size and Scale

The underlying agenda of district administration is for people to take risks, to be innovative, to be creative, to be looking forward and to be improving the instructional program. There are incentives built in for people to be looking in those directions.—An assistant superintendent

When I came here I thought I'd died and gone to heaven. This was such a lovely place. But we had such a repressive regime at the superintendent's level.—A former union president

We found that there are some people who haven't been in the union for years and years, maybe they've been in the school for almost 15, 16 years and never joined, you sort of forget about them, "oh that's old so-and-so, he'll never come in," so we'd start talking to the new teachers who've just been hired to see if they want to join, but to our surprise these people we thought were no good talking to, we're just wasting our breath, all of a sudden they're saying, "we'd like to join too." Some of them have mentioned the fact that things have changed.

—Special education department chair and
union representative

OAK VALLEY AND ITS TEACHERS

Oak Valley was an affluent California suburb that, between 1960 and 1990, was transformed from "kind of a back-woods town . . . kind of a country bumpkin place," according to a district administrator, into a community where "people moving out from the Midwest come to us with high demands and high expectations for the schools." Oak Valley attracted prospective teachers from all over the country. Oak Valley educators, from teachers to superintendent, exhibited a self-consciousness and pride in the district's reputation as "a leader and protagonist" for innovation, for its wealth of professional development opportunities for teachers, and for its attempts to encourage "educational excellence" through a decentralized management structure. Pervasive in conversations with teachers and administrators was a conception of teacher professionalism rooted in entrepreneurship, hard work, high expectations for students, and an awareness of current developments in the greater educational field. "The strength of the district is reflected in many ways," said the union president, "and one of them is that we probably have [a sizeable proportion of] teachers who are attuned to a larger educational world."

"Decisions should be made at the lowest possible level," read a district maxim. In the second half of the 1980s, even before these trends became popular elsewhere, Oak Valley teachers, not central office staff, were responsible for curriculum development and for the infusion and local dissemination of pedagogical innovation. Under the supervision of administrators, teams of teachers worked together across school sites to align coursework to state curriculum frameworks, approve new courses, and ensure course consistency across schools. About one-fifth of the district's teachers wrote proposals for competitive grants for funds to support curriculum development in their schools. Other teachers, funded by the California Mentor Teacher Program, developed curriculum projects to share with other teachers across the district. According to the former union president who negotiated how Mentor Teacher monies would be allocated in the district, the intent was to shift curricular authority from administrators' to teachers' hands. But it is clear that the administrators who approved Mentor Teacher proposals and encouraged the dissemination of particular projects were the real managers of the program and strongly influenced the tenor of curricular change within the district.

The district provided a wealth of staff development courses, with teachers leading the majority of workshops. District administrators believed that teachers presented at these events "for the prestige among peers and administrators," "to be on the inside, in the know," not for the additional pay, which was minimal. Yet just as teachers' involvement in "decisions made at the lowest possible level" depended on each school principal's willingness to include them, administrative control was a strong determinant of teachers' professional development. Administrators decided whom to fund to attend professional conferences, which staff development courses would be held in the district, and which teachers would be required to attend. What might be touted as "a program for teachers by teachers" was actually managed by district administrators.

In 1989, Oak Valley High was one of two district high schools. Interviews with teachers and administrators suggested a secondary school culture that seemed to turn inward, a marked contrast from the cosmopolitan view reflected in the remarks of district administrators and of teachers in other district schools. Oak Valley High teachers placed a strong value on relationships with students in their classrooms but exerted little energy to developing relationships with colleagues within the school or district. An English teacher described her colleagues as "so involved in curriculum and students that they'd rather someone else [served as union representative]." A new principal, wanting to introduce cross-disciplinary activities and other whole-school educational programs, marveled at the "conservative" nature of the faculty and teachers' lack of awareness of any activities outside of their departments.

Oak Valley High's sheer size effectively limited teachers' opportunities for interaction. With housing tracts continuing to expand and the district's student population still growing, a faculty of nearly 150 met over 3,000 students every day. Academic departments were so large that, as a science teacher said, "I hardly get to know the people in my department." Some teachers spoke of their departments as sources of social and intellectual support, but the number of new faculty in recent years resulted not only in departmental balkanization but also in factionalism within departmental units (see Siskin, 1994). At a rare full-school faculty meeting, even "an outsider could take a look and see the cliques. There's the math department. Oh, wait a second, there's cliques in the math department!"

School size also contributed to the difficulty of collegial interaction. Between departments teachers were "spread out in different buildings, there is no central area for teachers to meet and be together, the lunchroom is minute, and I know many people never set foot out of their classroom and department workrooms so I never get to know them." A social studies teacher described how "sometimes . . . we walk up to the office and meet up with people from across campus . . . [and we say] things like 'gosh, you still work here.'" A math teacher contrasted the district middle school where she taught years ago with what she experienced at Oak Valley High.

When I first came here, it was a shock, because [of] the relationship that we had with the teachers, the socializing that we had [at my old school]. When I came to Oak Valley High, there wasn't the camaraderie of the faculty, because they're off in our departments. . . . The first thing in the morning all the [middle school] teachers met in the faculty lounge, during the day when we had a prep all of the teachers were there, and after school that was the place to go to get the support of your fellow workers. At Oak Valley High, there's no place to go other than the resource center or your classroom or another teacher's classroom.

In the late 1970s, as delineated in Table 5.1, Oak Valley High had adopted an innovative curriculum where students worked through "learning modules" at their own pace. Teachers who weren't enthusiastic about the program were encouraged to transfer to the district's newly opened second high school. A veteran teacher recalled that the new curriculum "required 10 times more work than a normal teaching arrangement. So Oak Valley was left with a real strong [and committed] faculty." But the community grew uncomfortable with the lack of structure "because they associated bare school grounds with learning." After a few years of experimental courses and scheduling, the district intervened and imposed a conventional instructional format. Briefed on this history by district personnel, the principal who came to Oak Valley High in 1990 was led to understand that

Things got out of hand . . . tremendous opportunities but kids were standing around outside the school during school hours and people were getting ticked off . . . a lack of supervision, lack of details . . . so they brought in [a new principal] to clean it up and . . . they got rid of a whole bunch of [teachers] and things became back in control.

Oak Valley underwent a deliberate normative transformation. While some teachers chose to leave, according to a district administrator, "some [40–50%] are still here, some saw the school becoming better and jumped on the bandwagon—the silent majority." Veteran teachers interviewed in 1989 recalled the transition period, and the 10 years following, as an era of administrative "heavy-handedness," with school administrators carrying out what were clearly district directives. A social studies teacher said she "knew what it was like to live under totalitarianism."

There was a lot of conflict between this department and the administration. They zeroed in on us and for some reason they decided to . . . destroy the morale. It wasn't just this department, it was school-wide. And we went through some bad times. . . .

TABLE 5.1 Salient events, Oak Valley High School

YEAR	UNION	DISTRICT	SCHOOL
1962		3,000 students	School opens
1969			Student-paced curriculum initiated
1972	6-member AFT chapter organized		
1974		Second high school opens	
1975		New supt. 12,000 students	
1976	Collective bargaining law passed in California. AFT wins election with 19% membership		
1977	First contract negotiated		
1979			Unit system disbanded; school "cleaned up"
1981	"Almost strike"		Faculty Advisory Council formed
1984	"Almost strike;" 69% membership	Mentor Teacher Program negotiated	
1985		Oak Valley Colloquium begins	Vice principal during "clean up" becomes principal
1987	First collaborative project. Current pres. elected		
1989	Current pres. reelected. Non-adversarial bargaining. 80% membership	23,000 students; 900 teachers	New principal. 3,150 students; 147 teachers. 50% union membership
1990	Collaborative project expanded and second considered		60% union membership
1991		Third high school projected	
1995		33,000 students projected	

You didn't want to make waves, you didn't want to say anything
because it would become repressive, you would be punished
some way or another. You would have to teach a course you
didn't want to teach, or you would be taken out of your department. . . . You retreated into your department and into yourself.

The tenor of administrative control over teachers' professional interactions, combined with a pattern of administrative patronage and
internal promotions up the administrative ladder from school to district office, meant that teachers' reputations, both as individuals and as
a school faculty, were transmitted up and down the district hierarchy
and endured over time. The new principal discovered that "there's some
views about [particular] teachers that have been allowed to stay that way
for 12 years. [As a result,] a lot of creative people on this campus have
been stifled."

THE UNION IN CONTEXT

The characterization of administrative "heavy-handedness" and
"favoritism" at the school level paralleled an enduring pattern of
adversarial relations between district administrators and teachers. In the
early 1970s, for example, the superintendent sent a letter to the first
president of the Oak Valley Federation of Teachers (OVFT) that read, in
part, "I am the superintendent, you are a teacher; I give the directives,
you carry them out." In a district that already enjoyed a reputation for
good teachers, such authoritarian actions were particularly rankling.

During the 1970s and 1980s, as in many other districts, teachers'
salaries and other material benefits were the major points of contention
between teachers and the district. As in other contexts, teachers considered economic benefits, whatever their real value, as proxies for how
well they were supported and respected. This linkage of issues is illus-
trated in the comments of an Oak Valley High union representative.

I've gone to the [union] meetings and I've heard all the little
grievances and the problems and the stupid things that principals do and get away with unless the union says, "You can't do
that," and then you really see the need for the union. You've got
an outstanding district and the superintendent says, "We have
great teachers!" But they weren't paying anything comparable
even to the other districts. They still aren't. We still aren't the
top paid district and yet we get all the accolades. It doesn't make

any sense to me. And we're a rich district that could afford to pay it, you would think.

Given the degree of contention between teachers and administrators, one might assume that the union played a significant role in teachers' collective identity and in their relationships with administrators. Indeed, across the district, according to the union president, "almost all of our teachers will go picket"; but at Oak Valley High, according to the senior union representative, during the most recent union action, in 1987, "maybe a third of our teachers were participating. The rest were ignoring it. Or deliberately staying out of it." In contrast to the district overall, where just under 80% of the teachers were union members, Oak Valley High's membership rate was barely 50%. Oak Valley High teachers' assessments of the strength of union commitment across the faculty were inconsistent and not necessarily accurate. Even the senior union representative had to count off names on a list before she could say what the school's membership profile looked like. "[Union commitment is] very strong," one nonmember believed. A second union representative characterized the faculty's level of union commitment as

. . . a mixture. Certain faces come to mind of individuals who are very, very strong union and whatever we ask they're willing to do. Others are just members because they know the union will back them. And others, it's like no real strong feelings.

The sheer size and organization of the school inhibited the kinds of communication and social cohesion across departmental lines that could encourage a strong union profile at other schools, like Rancho. Departments might be hubs of union affiliation, depending on the leadership of individuals within them and the extent to which union issues, or potential union issues, had important implications for instruction. For example, the daily course schedule might be most salient to the teaching of a particular subject. But departments could also buffer teachers from the union: A foreign language teacher, for example, could say she didn't "feel any pressure because I have no exposure to militant teachers." Finally, departmentalization could be a deterrent to the efficiency of the union in the school. Ten years earlier, the union president became aware "that you couldn't have one building rep [at Oak Valley High]. I had a rep in every department. And so I had like a council of reps there." Even with an increase in the allowable number of representative positions, however, in 1989 most departments did not have a union representative.

There were no formal opportunities for teachers to contact union representatives. And with no common meeting place, teachers had to grab a union representative

> . . . on the run. They catch me when I'm at the ditto machine or the library or the ladies' room, wherever it is that I happen to be. . . . You have to search each other out. If they're on your mind, and you want to get back to them, you hope you pass each other again. I saw one teacher yesterday at the district office and I know that he was [having a problem] and I wanted to talk with him a bit. And the time wasn't there, so I'll try to catch him another time.

It took some time for a new group of teachers to replace the first generation of union activists who had played a prominent role when the OVFT first organized in the district in 1976. During much of the 1980s, teachers tended to sign on for a union rep position one year at a time, and the school typically lacked its full complement in union council meetings. District-level union leadership believed that "a strong union thrives at the lowest level with strong rank and file," but Oak Valley High's union strength was limited by a tradition of site-level union representatives who understood their role as conduits rather than teacher leaders. Many micro-political problems that could have been resolved by effective site-level intervention instead were referred directly to the union president. This tradition of concentrating authority in one strong union leader created strong associations for teachers between "the union" and the actions of particular past presidents. In 1989, for example, a teacher could still recall the president's response during the height of the school's "totalitarian" period 10 years before.

> We called [the union] when we were having some problems, we brought in the leader of the union. We voiced some of our concerns to him and we never heard from him again. He's now an administrator for the district. . . . He was playing both sides. At that time I withdrew from the union.

Commitment to the union was also weakened by a dissonance between teachers' political "conservatism" and the union's "labor practices." In 1976, with the advent of collective bargaining in the state, the Oak Valley Federation of Teachers, an AFT affiliate, won the local representation election when the reputedly less militant California Teachers' Association, perhaps the more "natural" choice for this district, "had not gotten a contract in a couple years, the leadership was real poor, and people were fed up." The OVFT was unabashedly Democratic in its politics and publicly supported other local labor groups. A veteran science teacher cited the union's politics as a major reason why he was not a member: "Every person they recommend voting for is a Democrat, every issue they recommend voting for I'm opposed to, and I'm a Republican, okay? And this is a Republican area."

Over the years, Oak Valley teachers routinely directed the union to emphasize material benefits over teachers' rights during collective bargaining sessions. Adversarial bargaining followed a predictable pattern. "You knew that about every 3 years you'd be out on the picket line in front of the school. And it always seemed like whenever we wanted any changes [there would be] brinkmanship, right to the edge every time and see who blinks." According to a union representative, it was

> . . . bargain, bargain, bargain for summer, September we come back [to school] with no contract, we had to raise the level of concern with the teachers to get the superintendent involved in the negotiations, we had to make it important for him to settle. Otherwise nothing would get done.

This pattern perpetuated an impression of the union as a "hard bargainer" in a district where teachers were sensitive to the fact that "administrators won't help us if they're bombarded."

Finally, many teachers identified with the rhetoric of teacher professionalism espoused by the administration—that hard work would be recognized and rewarded—and were uncomfortable with the union's adversarial tone. When teachers find a union inappropriate to their condition, they may invent or utilize other existing representative forums. At Oak Valley High, teachers created a Faculty Advisory Council to handle "the problems when teachers felt they couldn't go to the principal, or if they did [but] they got no action at all." Council members met with teachers, formally or informally, and then determined whether the issue warranted a conversation with the principal or another administrator. Advisory Council membership was "kind of pass-the-torch to somebody else in your department after a couple of years, very, very informal." Teachers could express their concerns "and not feel threatened. You must be a trustworthy person to serve." In 1990, Oak Valley High's new principal was calling this group "the unofficial but nonetheless real union" and invited its members to an occasional pizza dinner with him to serve "as a sounding board" for his ideas.

A second alternative form of representation, the Oak Valley

Colloquium, evolved out of the impasse between union and administration at the district level. The monthly lunch meeting of superintendent and a teacher representative from each school allowed the superintendent to feel he had his finger on the pulse of what was going on at the ground level. At the same time, according to Oak Valley High's Colloquium representative, it gave teachers a way to

> ... let [the superintendent] know that, all political stuff aside, these are concerns that we have. And if it is [an issue the union has already addressed in contract negotiations], he gets the message that hey, this isn't just the union looking for union rights, these are teachers saying "we've got a problem" and it sounds like a legitimate one.

THE "NEW" UNION

In the late 1980s, a major shift in union–administration dynamics had a marked effect on how Oak Valley High teachers thought about the union. The transformation from adversarial to cooperative labor relations was the result of several concurrent events and ideas. In 1987, a teacher representative to the Oak Valley Colloquium introduced the notion of nonadversarial bargaining to the superintendent and the district at large. At about the same time, the union and district cooperatively initiated a program for teachers new to the district that included peer coaching and assessment, professional development, and other forms of support. In the process of developing the terms of agreement for this project, the union and district administration "began to form different perceptions of each other. . . . We were not ogres on either side as long as we were talking about issues for which we had a general concern for resolution." The union president decided to run for an unprecedented second consecutive term, "and the superintendent finally took notice of him. As a power. As somebody he had to deal with." During the summer of 1989, the union president and superintendent left the district with a facilitator for several days, and, according to the president,

> We really got down to what the problems were. The district had never recognized the legitimacy of the union in representing the teachers. And out of that came some agreements about how we would behave toward each other and an agreement to try and conclude the next round of contract negotiations on a win–win

basis. And we did have a very excellent negotiation, and because we agreed we would address each issue on its own merits and not link issues to condition of agreements on other things, we disposed of a dozen issues that probably had been rankling both sides for 10 or 12 years.

Teachers noticed the change. In 1989 Oak Valley High teachers had perceived "cynicism in the way negotiations are being carried out . . . a lack of respect for each side," but by the next year union membership began to grow, slowly but noticeably, to over 80% district-wide, and above 60% at Oak Valley High. The senior representative reported that "some of the old teachers that haven't been union members for 20 years have joined because of this nonadversarial bargaining. They really are pleased." A veteran teacher who had objected to OVFT politics in the past joined the union because of what he saw as "a strong moral stand on a couple of issues, which I really appreciate." Typical of teachers' pride in the district's reputation for innovation was this comment by an Oak Valley union representative, who believed that "our union will be looked at as a model of maybe how to get around some of this [adversarial] stuff, and it is. There are people coming in from all over the country to study these nonadversarial dealings."

Teachers were more likely than before to turn to the union when they felt a need for job protection. More often than before, according to a union representative, "teachers [are] coming up to me and saying 'You're a union rep, what does the union say about this, have you taken it up with the union, what's the word, make sure they know about it, make sure they know we're not happy about it.'" In 1990, a half dozen teachers were curious enough about "the thinking of the district, the difference between the teachers and the administration," that for the first time in a number of years Oak Valley High had a full complement of union representatives regularly attending meetings.

By virtue of its new relationship with district administration, the union was increasingly successful in representing teachers' interests. Union leaders as well as the teachers involved in the new programs were members of influential district committees and found their opinions and expertise were valued. As in other districts undergoing shifts in labor relations, it was possible to resolve potentially conflictual issues more quickly and easily. The union and teachers' new prominence in district-level decision making led to a number of changes in district procedures, allocation of resources, professional development opportunities for teachers, and improvements in working relationships.

TEACHERS' PROFESSIONAL COMMUNITY
AND THE FEDERATION

As a campus and a culture, Oak Valley High provided little in the way of collegial encounters for teachers. As a substitute, because they identified strongly with the recognition the district received for innovative programs and quality education, teachers relied on a generalized sense of community in the district as a whole. Even those who were sensitive to administrators' tendencies to "run rough-shod" over teachers, believed the solution lay in administrative recognition of teachers' contributions to quality programs. Teachers based their commitment to the Federation on their beliefs in the "moral" utility of the union to that broader conception of professional community. In this context, many teachers understood the union's efforts to improve teachers' economic conditions as attempts to ensure administrative recognition. The increase in union membership once administration and union exhibited a more cooperative relationship appears to have been due to a new sense of district-wide solidarity. And as the union's representative function grew more effective, its practical utility for teachers grew as well.

Union representatives in particular discovered a commonality of purpose within the union organization that they did not experience within their own school. Representatives spoke about their roles as occasions for social involvement and affirmation of community: "I want to instill in other teachers that feeling about themselves, that we are very important people and what we do is very important," said one union representative. A science teacher found that while she could not always expect her school colleagues to be available, she could take issues "to the union" and get "their opinions and support." Another teacher said she found a "pure psychic satisfaction of working together with other teachers who you know are really committed to improving the teaching profession as a profession, working together for the good of fellow teachers. . . . And there's also the satisfaction of being able to feel useful to the teachers on campus."

These teachers, reflecting the entrepreneurial spirit and professional self-consciousness typical of other district "teacher leaders," saw the union as an important locus for professional interaction and development. Representatives had early knowledge of the new professional roles available to teachers through the peer assistance and staff development programs. The union also served as a source of important information: A representative could "hear the latest word, maybe some things that are coming up that we're going to have to watch out for in the future." The union, in short, could provide resourceful representatives with opportunities to move outward into a broader professional community.

The new collaboratively sponsored programs provided opportunities for a broader range of teachers to interact with other educational professionals. At the same time, they took professional development opportunities out of the exclusive domain of district administrators without excluding administrators entirely. The identification of project personnel was the joint purview of union leaders, other respected teachers, and district administrators. This nonpartisan coalition did much to reinforce the notion that the new programs were consonant with teachers' conceptions of a district-wide professional community.

From 1989 to 1990, the Oak Valley Federation of Teachers became the catalyst for the formation of a professional community that held a strong practical as well as social value for Oak Valley High teachers. Teachers were able to shift from a position of powerlessness relative to administrators, where they had few opportunities to participate in the broader district community, to a position of greater political power, professional recognition, and professional support. The union was the key to this transformation, and teachers were well aware of its role in the change.

Chapter 6

The Social Value
of Teacher Unions

> We share a task: working with kids. There is a brotherhood,
> a sisterhood, whatever the particular nonsexist term is now
> for that kind of goings-on. And I look and say, OK, who are
> the other people who are on the other side?
> —A former Rancho social studies teacher

> I just feel, and maybe it's selfish in some ways, that I don't
> need the union.—An economics teacher at Onyx Ridge

> I guess I joined [the union because] I felt I wasn't doing my
> share, I'm not part of the majority here and maybe I should
> do more. Although I haven't taken advantage of any of the
> perks that come with union membership, there may be a
> degree of comfort in having them. That was not paramount.
> I don't even think I know what they are. . . . It's a conscience
> thing.—A science teacher at Oak Valley High

The three previous chapters describe three very different assessments
of the value of union strategies for teachers—assessments that are the
products of teachers' local, collective interpretations of a variety of
actions, events, conditions, and issues. The cases were written in a way
that emphasizes a consistency of meaning and logic among teachers
within any one school. It is important to acknowledge, however, that
each faculty actually encompassed a broad range of attitudes and levels
of commitment toward the local teacher union and toward teacher
unionism more generally.

In each school there were some teachers whose willingness to
assume union leadership positions could be taken for granted; some
teachers whose union involvement was minimal, intermittent, or ambivalent; and some teachers who did not contribute or participate in union-

related activities in any way. At Rancho, for example, where faculty commitment to the Teachers' Association was so pervasive that only three teachers reported to school during a one-day "sick-out" organized by other teachers, an English teacher could still claim that "my level of involvement is about zero." Even at Onyx Ridge, where the Teachers' Association had least salience among the three schools, a math teacher could be strongly pro-union: "[My] family is union, and there was just never even a decision." Concerned about stretching herself too thin across multiple commitments and unwilling to assume an official leadership position, this teacher nonetheless felt "a lot of respect for anyone who takes on the responsibility to do those things. So I just told [the union representative], 'If I can do anything to help, I'd be most happy to.'"

TEACHERS' ACCOUNTS OF THE VALUE OF UNIONISM

An earlier line of research on teacher unions looked for relationships between teachers' level of political militancy—their willingness to strike, for example, or to challenge administrative authority—and demographic characteristics such as age and gender that teachers independently "brought to school" (see, for example, Cole, 1968; Corwin, 1970; Lowe, 1965). To what extent might the value teachers found in unionism be the product of factors originating outside of the school, and to what extent did teachers' perspectives appear to be shaped by the conditions of their work? Table 6.1 presents the actual explanations Rancho, Onyx Ridge, and Oak Valley teachers provided when asked to account for their levels of union involvement and commitment.

A small number of teachers' explanations appear to reflect their own idiosyncratic conditions. Some, like that of the Onyx Ridge math teacher cited earlier, referred to a family perspective on unionism. Some teachers identified a particular action or event as a critical incident: An especially memorable episode, such as a conflict with an administrator or a strike, provided the formative basis for a particular perspective on the nature or value of teacher unionism. In these cases, the critical incident usually occurred during the first few years of teaching and referred to situations and interpretations teachers did not necessarily share with colleagues. Teachers at the same school may have lived through the same sequence of events, but the cases suggest that not all teachers responded in the same way or with the same intensity.

Some teachers offered explanations that emphasized an abstract or philosophical position rather than referring to particular conditions or

TABLE 6.1 Teachers' Explanations of Level
of Union Commitment

RANCHO Teacher ID#	Union Attitude	Type(s) of Explanation	Explanation
RA021	In favor	Critical incident	As a new teacher in another district, he was assigned extra duties by his principal and was taken to court for breaking up a fight between a teacher and student. "It was at this point that I began feeling a need for representation."
RA033	In favor	Family Economic	"Basically I'm from a union family. My father stressed the virtues of union. And I have favorable opinions of them in general . . . I guess I look at it as something you have to do to benefit financially."
RA065	In favor	Workplace	"The science department is very strong in the union." At lunch with the other science teachers, talk was of contract problems, problems with the communication system. "The more I found out, the angrier I got." "The Teachers' Association is a rational way of solving problems."
RA038	Moderate	Workplace Social	"I am a [union] member, yes. I'm not real pleased with it but there's a lot of unsettled feelings about what goes on downtown . . . The last time we went on strike, I went on strike because I didn't want to deal with the hassles if I didn't."
RA003	Opposed	Workplace Principled	"Although I can theoretically see the necessity for unions, it's very adversarial . . . There's no point to that kind of relationship between administrators and teachers. And with a few exceptions, the people who have been involved in the union are not people I admire."
RA029	Opposed	Social Principled	"As it got closer to whether we would strike, I kept saying to myself, 'I've got to work with these people, I need their support, and they took a risk and went on strike and that will benefit me as well,' and I think that when all is said, I would go on strike next time, I would do it. And I would set aside any personal conviction I had about whether or not striking is right or wrong. And I don't believe it's right."

TABLE 6.1 (*continued*)

ONYX RIDGE Teacher ID#	Union Attitude	Type(s) of Explanation	Explanation
OR006	In favor	Family Principled	"When I started teaching it was assumed teachers are professionals and belong to professional organizations, [not] coerced, but expected. And my family is union, and there was never even a decision."
OR047	In favor	Critical incident	"My first school is where I got involved . . . We had problems with the principal in that probationary teachers seemed picked on. I started complaining to the Teachers' Association and naively said yes when they asked whether anyone on campus wanted to [be involved]."
OR018	Moderate	Workplace Principled	"[The union is] an organization where people can take individual grievances. They're there as a backup, which maybe makes it sound like I'm not a strong member, and perhaps I'm not, because I think the assignments I've had have been very fortunate."
OR044	Moderate	Principled	"The union is just something that I belong to, but I'm not involved with it really . . . It's there and it's nice to know that it's there in terms of looking out for teachers and their needs and concerns."
OR010	Opposed	Critical incident Principled	"When I signed my contract, I asked [the union] about credit for military service and they said, 'Oh, we've eliminated that.' I didn't join the union because they neglected an individual . . . I would have joined if they had given me satisfaction and gotten back to me and explained their position. At that point I was right there on the fence."
OR016	Opposed	Principled	"[One] of the reasons I don't believe in unions is that money was just never a factor [in my decision to be a teacher] . . . I never felt their issues were anything I could identify with."
OR052	Opposed	Principled	"I just feel that I couldn't always comply with what the union wanted us to do, and I didn't feel that I could be a member that was worthy of what they thought a member should be."

TABLE 6.1 (*continued*)

OAK VALLEY Teacher ID#	Union Attitude	Type(s) of Explanation	Explanation
OV006	In favor	Critical incident Principled	"The first year I ever taught, we almost had a strike. I thought, 'What have I gotten myself into?' . . . I hated the antagonism between the union and the administration. I got in the union because I wanted to see if maybe there was some way to change that . . . My family is aghast that I'm a union rep, but if you're going to change something you have to get on the inside."
OV031	In favor	Critical incident	"My first year I was absolutely shocked. There I was, a probationary teacher, and in October they were talking about calling a teachers' strike . . . I decided to be a rep [because] I wanted to find out the real workings of the Oak Valley district."
OV112	In favor	Family	"I've always supported the union very strongly. My family is working class, very strong union. Last year I suddenly realized that now's the time [to serve as union rep]."
OV130	In favor	Workplace	She first became a union rep because of "the attitude that the superintendent had towards teachers." Her current interest in being a rep is "to give support to teachers who have issues that come up in their professional lives that are overlooked."
OV027	In favor	Social Principled	"I joined this year because [the union president] took a strong moral stand on some issues, which I appreciated . . . I felt a sense of not doing my fair share. Although I haven't taken advantage of any of the perks . . . It's a conscience thing."
OV140	Moderate/ opposed	Principled	He joined for the first time this year in support of the union president for the cordial relationship he has been able to achieve. He may resign next year: he doesn't approve of unions.
OV014	Opposed	Critical incident Principled	She first taught in a school district where there was "a militant aggressive union," and doesn't see the union in Oak Valley as being a positive force. "It is tied to the national organization which supports political candidates I wouldn't support."

events. In these instances, the distinction between individual attribute and social construction is less clear. Teachers' beliefs or attitudes may have been formed independently of school and district context, but, as the Rancho and Onyx Ridge cases suggest—and as any teacher who finds him- or herself in philosophical opposition to the norm can attest—administrative attempts to recruit certain types of teachers to a school imply that teachers' shared values can be construed as conditions of teachers' work, and emerging workplace issues or events can serve to reinforce teachers' beliefs. Teachers' explanations that emphasized economic issues are similarly difficult to characterize as either purely individual or collectively shared because, as the cases attest, the value of salary and other personal benefits not only seemed a function of teachers' personal economic conditions but also reflected teachers' shared understandings of how well they were valued and supported by administrators, school board, and community.

Still other accounts reflect an awareness of colleagues' occupational interests or, in a different vein, what amounts to a perception of social pressure or coercion—clearly social dimensions to teachers' decisions about their level of union commitment. Finally, some explanations specifically reference workplace conditions: the ongoing relationships among teachers and administrators, for example, or teachers' concerns about class size or instructional resources.

What kinds of patterns are suggested by these accounts? First, teachers with stronger positions on teacher unionism in general and the local union in particular, whether "in favor" or "opposed," were more likely than teachers with "moderate" positions to provide an explanation that fell into one of the categories toward the "individual" end of the continuum, although this is not true across the board. Teachers who served as union representatives, for example, did not all claim union family backgrounds; nor did they all identify union organizing activities or other union-associated events as critical incidents.

Many teachers across all levels of union commitment provided more than one kind of explanation. Many teachers who gave individual types of accounts went on to speak about their level of union commitment in terms of current working conditions or events. Teachers' tendencies to provide combinations of explanations suggest interactions among whatever attitudes and beliefs they brought to their decisions and shared interpretations of events and issues salient to their work lives. This interaction among types of accounts does not reflect an arbitrary convergence of influences, however. The case studies demonstrate how the value of union presence and membership for teachers corresponds logically to the combination of features that constitute their workplaces. Teachers' conceptions of themselves as professionals, their relationships with colleagues and others, their perceptions of who supported and who impeded their work, and the values they shared form a logical fit. Teachers viewed local union strategies in relation to this fit because the union was, after all, one of the many dimensions of teachers' work lives.

Finally, there are consistencies within and differences between schools in the types of accounts teachers gave. Rancho teachers were more likely than teachers at the other two schools to consider economic, workplace, or social issues—explanations at the collective end of the spectrum; Onyx Ridge teachers were least likely to cite collective explanations; and Oak Valley teachers fell somewhere in between, but closer to Onyx Ridge than to Rancho. There are clear relationships between the kinds of explanations teachers gave and the strength and dimensionality of their relationships with their school colleagues.

UNIONS AND TEACHERS' PROFESSIONAL COMMUNITIES

Despite the number of depictions of teachers' work as inherently independent or isolated (see, for example, Hargreaves, 1993; Huberman, 1993; Little, 1993; Lortie, 1975; Sizer, 1984), there are strong social dimensions to teachers' work. Teachers not only spend most of their school hours with students, but they also interact with administrators, staff, and colleagues both within and across academic departments. Teachers "discover" and construct their professional communities around available opportunities for interaction, observations of common educational purpose, and needs for practical assistance, intellectual engagement, and social involvement. The composition of a professional community (*who* teachers recognize as "one of us") and the common values around which it forms (*what* "we" are trying to accomplish) provide the bases for understanding the value of union strategies in social terms.

The three case studies demonstrate how the opportunities and qualities inherent to teachers' professional interactions vary from one school setting to the next. Union leadership's understandings about the quality of teachers' professional interactions and the expressed values by which the union's actions are accounted for may match the professional community "map" within a particular school setting—or they may not. For example, union strategies at the district level may be predicated on an assumption of an animosity between teachers and school administrators that does not exist within the context of a particular school. Encountering and interacting with professional community characteristics, teacher unions can serve to intensify teachers' identification with their community, perform a valued but well-bounded function, or miss the point entirely.

Because of the complexity of teachers' work lives, teachers in the same schools may actually identify with a variety of forms of professional community. Other studies conducted in these and other schools reveal the intellectual, practical, and social significance for teachers of academic departments within schools (Johnson, 1990; Siskin, 1994; Siskin & Little, 1995) and, for a smaller number of teachers, of subject area and other special interest organizations across schools (Carter, 1991; Lichtenstein, McLaughlin, & Knudsen, 1992; Lord, 1991; Smith, 1991). In many schools, more informal groupings of teachers meet to talk about students and instruction.

The local union can be a focus for professional community for a sub-group of teachers in a school. At Rancho, union membership was a pervasive component of teachers' professional identification, especially for teacher leaders—"academic" as well as other kinds of activists. Onyx Ridge's lone union representative, a former union officer, had a special historic link with the Teachers' Association that predated and appeared stronger than his identification with his current school colleagues. Union representatives at Oak Valley described their roles as a special opportunity to interact with and to receive the support of other teachers across the district. In this and other districts where unions have sponsored professional development activities, unions can be a valued site for teacher learning, colleagueship, and a means for "contributing to the profession" for the teachers most directly involved (Bascia, 1991; Lieberman & Bascia, 1990).

When we shift our focus to the most prominent forms of professional community within any school context, however, the three cases provide strikingly different examples of the "fit" between important features of those professional communities and the value teachers ascribe to their unions. At Rancho, where the Teachers' Association had long been part of the fabric of teachers' sense of "who we are," the quality and frequency of teachers' social interactions allowed for an awareness of colleagues' personal as well as occupational issues; at Rancho, it was difficult to disentangle teachers' commitment to the Teachers' Association from feelings of collegial obligation and loyalty or from teachers' perceptions of collective personal and professional needs going unmet. In contrast, Onyx Ridge teachers' comments suggest that they chose Teachers' Association membership on the basis of personal values and their calculation, for themselves as individuals, of the importance of supporting an agent whose primary value was a form of "insurance" against potential inequities targeted at individual teachers. Teachers'

Association strategies were not consistent with teachers' sense of themselves as professionals or with their most valued form of professional community, their affiliation with other teachers around subject-based curricular issues. At Oak Valley, because of the lack of social cohesion within the school, teachers based their commitment to the Federation partly on independently held values and partly on shared beliefs in the "moral" utility of the Federation to a professional community that encompassed the whole district, including administrators.

The three cases suggest that a teacher union can perform a variety of roles in relation to the most prominent forms of teachers' professional community within a school. A union can help form, focus, bound, enhance, or extend community by identifying or reinforcing issues around which community members find commonality. Where this congruence is missing, a union will lack relevance to the professional community, and teachers' commitment to the local union will reflect idiosyncratic preferences rather than choices that are socially valued and reinforced.

Union Strategies at the Professional Community Level

Teacher unions attempt to ensure that their political actions are consistent with teachers' concerns. One strategy is the presence of at least one elected union representative at each site. Another is seeking teachers' opinions with regard to bargaining issues and potentially controversial actions such as strikes. Despite these precautions, however, as the three cases demonstrate, the responsiveness of teachers' organizations cannot be taken for granted. In situations where district-level concerns are out of synch with the conditions and issues of a particular school faculty, there may be differences between teachers' values and occupational needs and issues of relevance to union leaders. These differences are probably more likely in larger districts; this was the case at Onyx Ridge in Adobe Viejo, the largest of the three districts.

School faculties in the same district may easily reflect different professional community maps, despite the common influence of district-level practices. The representativeness of union actions becomes a less straightforward matter where teachers' professional identity is based on perceptions of values that distinguish them from others, rather than those which they hold in common. By addressing issues more consistent with professional community values or concerns at other schools, the Adobe Viejo Teachers' Association ran the risk of alienating Onyx Ridge teachers.

A teachers' professional community that is formed according to hierarchical distinctions is more likely to find value in the union's strategies where a union emphasizes hierarchical issues. At Rancho, teachers' perceptions of authority relations were a critical aspect of their sense of professional community and their common concerns paralleled the Teachers' Association's issues. For teachers at Onyx Ridge, on the other hand, where organizational or hierarchical levels were less relevant features of teachers' professional identities or working conditions, union strategies that emphasized traditional authority relations were not particularly compelling.

Finally, the overrepresentation of members of a particular teacher interest group can restrict the ability of other teachers to recognize a union as a viable mechanism for participation in decision making. At Rancho, most union representatives belonged to one of two academic departments, and teachers' discomfort with the perceived power imbalance among departments was only outweighed by the seriousness of their differences with district administration. At Oak Valley, a new cohort of teachers were moved to volunteer for union representative positions when it became clear that important scheduling decisions that affected their work were being made by union representatives from middle schools, whose priorities and needs differed from theirs.

Union leadership concerned with creating conditions that encourage teacher commitment must pay attention not only to teachers' practical needs but to the history and patterns of valued relationships and beliefs that contribute to local forms of professional community at the school level. These points are elaborated further in Chapter 8.

Chapter 7

The Practical Value of Teacher Unions

A couple [of teachers] have come up to me and said, "So-and-so has made a number of comments that they feel they're being dumped on," and so then one of us [union representatives] will go by and ferret out some more information. In some of those cases, I will unofficially go in and talk with the appropriate administrator and say, "So-and-so is concerned. At this point they have not signed any formal grievance or complaint papers. Maybe it would be wise to go out and see if you can solve the problem before they get too frustrated." And I would say that 95% of the time the problem gets solved. I'll usually check back with the person and they'll say, "Yeah, things are working out, things are better."

—Rancho senior union representative

If teachers have a dispute they don't go to [the Teachers' Association representative]; they come to me. It's a matter of personality and position, and because we have a large segment of the faculty who are not union members.

—Onyx Ridge principal

I am union leadership. By the fact that I go to the executive meetings. [The union president] and the executive board can do nothing unless all the reps vote on it. They don't have any legal power. So I am actually making policy by being there, listening to the information, and making recommendations by my vote. And sometimes I think the staff members don't realize that we are their representatives, we are their voice, and if they don't make their feelings known to us, we have to do it with our own best judgment. Sometimes that's with rather limited background knowledge.

—Oak Valley senior union representative

THE SALIENCE OF TRADITIONAL UNION ISSUES

Rancho, Onyx Ridge, and Oak Valley teachers expected their unions to assume defensive roles with respect to issues of job protection, instructional resources, and personal economic benefits, and to provide a vehicle for teachers' representative participation in educational decision making. These expectations are consistent with findings reported in other historical and recent research on teacher unionism. But while much of the literature has criticized teachers for the "narrowness" of their concerns, citing teachers as "conservative" rather than "professional" (Johnson, 1983, 1984; McDonnell & Pascal, 1988; Urban, 1982), or charged union leaders with framing educational issues in "economic" and "political" rather than academic terms (Kerchner & Mitchell, 1986; Mitchell & Kerchner, 1983; Simpkins, McCutcheon, & Alec, 1979), this chapter elaborates the reasons why traditional union issues remain relevant and legitimate concerns for teachers.

Teachers at Rancho, Onyx Ridge, and Oak Valley called upon the union when they believed it was warranted by the conditions of their work. Differences in collective agreements, the relative historical success or failure of union intervention, local conceptions of teaching, and professional community characteristics provided the criteria by which teachers decided when union intervention was appropriate. The first sections of the chapter describe how these contextual differences determined the actual uses to which teachers put their union with respect to issues of job protection and representation. Despite these differences between cases, however, teachers across schools and even teachers with different attitudes toward unions tended to subscribe to an at least hypothetical need for unions against what they understood as inappropriate control by others over their work. The discussions that follow consider why teachers' expectations for union intervention remain so pervasive, by exploring features of the policy environment in which unions function, the relationship between contractual provisions and teacher expectations, and the institutional contexts in which teachers work.

Job Protection

Workload. Teachers turned to their union when they believed their classes were too large, too long, or too many; when administrators required that they assume extra work during assigned planning periods, at lunch, or after school; or when they were assigned to courses, subjects, or schools for which they felt they lacked competence and could not perform well. One of teachers' major concerns was equity; another was a manageable and satisfying work load.

Teachers felt particularly entitled to call for union intervention where contract provisions existed with respect to a particular issue. Rancho teachers, for example, working with the most extensive and well-specified collective agreement of the three schools, could and would challenge a proposal that district high schools move from a 5- to a 6-period day, on the grounds that "it would be 17% more work because you'd have that many more papers to grade." At the same time, whether their contract reflected it or not, teachers at all three schools agreed about some areas over which they should have some legal control. Oak Valley teachers, for example, believed the Federation should be able to intervene in the case of undesired transfers from one district school to another, and teachers at Onyx Ridge believed the Teachers' Association should be able to "do something about class size." On the other hand, Onyx Ridge teachers' conception of teaching as requiring whatever it took to get the job done and done well meant that, in this context, teachers would not readily invoke the union over work-load issues. Even the alternate union representative found that "there's always something that you feel you're not doing that you should be doing in education, right?"

Health and safety. Teachers at all three schools expected union involvement in situations where their own or students' physical well-being was threatened. At Rancho, teachers lobbied through the union for a communications system between classrooms and the main office in case of sudden illness or danger. At Onyx Ridge and Oak Valley, filing a grievance was the routine procedure to report a health or safety issue. An Onyx Ridge social studies teacher mentioned

> . . . a grievance on file I think from 2 or 3 years after the school was built having to [do] with the air conditioning system, which is terrible. The teachers got together and filed a suit, I mean we had one teacher who has asthma and it really does create some problems. And yet what is everybody going to do, walk out and say, "We're not coming back until it's fixed"?

Legal representation. Teachers recognized the union as their legal representative when they felt unfairly treated or accused by administrators, students, parents, or other teachers. Even at Onyx Ridge, where the Teachers' Association's purview was especially limited and teachers would have been particularly embarrassed by charges of incompetence,

there were numerous occasions when teachers requested legal representation—including teachers who were not union members.

Economic Issues

Some teachers found the economic issues with which their unions
were concerned inherently distinct from the central activities of teaching and learning. A Rancho union representative contrasted his work as
department chair, where "you're cooperative, you try to work in a man-
ner that tries to meet everybody's needs," with his union involvement,
which he considered "much more a selfish self-interest thing . . . though
there's some overlap [with issues that affect the quality of work]." A nonunion member at Onyx Ridge asserted that "I never complained about the
money. That's one of the reasons I don't believe in unions. Money wasn't
a factor [in choosing a teaching career]." But other teachers saw strong connections between economic issues—material resources for teaching as
well as personal salary and benefits—and other conditions of their work.

Instructional resources. Teachers called for union intervention when
a lack of materials interfered with their ability to teach according to their
professional standards. Because the parent community raised funds
to supplement monies the school received from the district, material
resources were not union issues at Onyx Ridge. At Rancho and Oak Valley, however, material resource issues dominated the collective bargaining landscape. At Oak Valley, with principals responsible for determin-
ing how school funds would be allocated, administrative control was
the salient issue. In the Mostaza district, according to Rancho's senior
union representative,

> People called it a laundry list, lots of issues that a lot of us who
> had been in the district a long time thought should never have
> been on the negotiating table: mirrors for the speech therapists
> [for example]. I mean you're talking about a maybe $100–$200
> expenditure. There were some issues that dealt with very small
> numbers of people. Over a 5- or 6-year period, people got more
> and more frustrated and eventually this list grew to about 125
> issues. In a district with a budget the size that it is I am sure you
> could have easily found [that amount of money] in some area.
> They could have solved that. But it had become we and they.

Personal benefits. For many teachers, a district's provision or restric-
tion of personal economic benefits carried symbolic weight greater than

seemed warranted by practical value alone. Onyx Ridge teachers' dis-
avowal of a relationship between remuneration and professional stat-
ure suggests they recognized the salience of linkage for other teachers,
even in their own district, even while they challenged its value according to their own standards. At Rancho and Oak Valley, teachers perceived
district unwillingness to agree to a salary increase as evidence of a lack
of recognition of their professional worth. Rather than identifying a particular salary level necessary for economic survival or comfort, teachers
tended to assess their income against salaries in other districts, or those
of other occupational groups, referencing issues of professional status,
recognition, and expertise.

Representative Participation
in Educational Decision Making

In ideal terms, as legal representatives unions can be "the means
by which an occupational community can monopolize and protect areas
of expertise" (Van Maanen & Barley, 1984). In practice, however, the
actual range of issues over which unions have legal purview is limited:
Unions command less occupational authority than do the organizations
that represent the so-called professionalized occupations, such as law
and medicine (Haberman, 1986; Olson, 1965; see also Carlson, 1992;
Larson, 1977; Sykes, 1986, 1987).

Niches and gaps. At the three schools in this study, unions served as
conduits for teachers' contributions to decisions that affected their work.
But other options were also available: Teachers participated in educational decision making, directly or through representatives, in departmental settings, school- and district-level advisory councils and committees, and through personal contacts with administrators and other
decision makers. Access to these other options, the important features
of the predominant professional community, the historical role of the
union in responding to teachers' concerns, and the personalities and
leadership styles of particular individuals all shaped teachers' views of
the union's viability as a representative forum for their concerns and
ideas. These cases illustrate how, by virtue of their particular strengths
and limitations, the unions filled representation "niches" around other
forms of representation as well as creating "gaps" that were filled by other
forms of access and participation. In the absence of other forms of representation, teachers might find it necessary to invent a union. But the
actual "representation profile" particular to a union was fundamentally
a local phenomenon.

The "Rancho Plan" of participatory governance was in many senses "of the union." It first attracted teachers for whom the Teachers' Association was a complementary vehicle: Many Teachers' Association representatives were also department, council, and committee chairs; many school issues were potential union issues; and union sensitivities held a prominent place in school decision making. Later, when Rancho's representative mechanisms were rendered ineffective by the district's refusal to let teachers make school decisions and the Teachers' Association request for a "work to rule" resulted in teachers' refusal to attend meetings, teachers and lost faith in the productivity of their collective efforts. Traditionally a conduit for teachers to school administration, the senior building representative performed an increasingly crucial role as teachers turn to him even at times when "they could have approached the administrator directly." Where once the Teachers' Association was one of a number of integrated and overlapping opportunities for teacher involvement in decision making, it later became one of only a few legitimate forms of access for teachers.

At Onyx Ridge, on the other hand, teachers were involved in school decision making through their membership on a variety of committees, and many regularly contributed to district and regional curriculum development committee work. A council of department chairs served as the principal's advisory group and contributed to decisions about schoolwide issues such as resource allocations. The Teachers' Association representative and principal maintained a "cordial" relationship, but teachers turned directly to administrators rather than employing the Teachers' Association representative as a go-between. The Teachers' Association contributed little to teacher participation in decision making, and teachers found little necessity for a more prominent role for the union.

Oak Valley teachers created union-like alternatives when the official union proved unworkable. At other district schools, "unit building committees" established by the union a decade earlier remained active forums for school-wide decision making, but at Oak Valley High, the Federation's historical failure to address teachers' work issues, and some amount of ambivalence toward union politics, led to the formation of a Faculty Advisory Council that brought teachers' work concerns to administrators' attention. Similarly, at the district level, the Oak Valley Colloquium was an alternative vehicle for communication between teacher representatives and the superintendent. More recently, the Federation's greater effectiveness and increased involvement in district policy setting enhanced its viability as a form of teacher representation at the district level. At the school, however, the size of the faculty, the departmentalized nature of teachers' work lives, and the school's only partial, recent emergence from an ethos of teacher isolation all rendered teachers' access to decision-making bodies piecemeal.

Teacher leadership. Social acknowledgment of one's actions can serve as a powerful incentive for teachers' contributions to the collective good (Olson, 1965). While other leadership positions (academic department or committee chairships, for example) might reflect collegial or administrative recognition of a teacher's special talent, however, union representation at Rancho, Onyx Ridge, and Oak Valley was neither a high status nor a high profile job. In these schools, without exception, teachers who served as union representatives ran unopposed for office, and, except in times of overt conflict, teachers were "barely aware" of who their current representatives were. At the same time, the extent of teachers' contributions to unionism is well worth noting. While some teachers "tried out" a union representative position for a single year, others served continuously in these roles for many terms; still others were intermittently involved, concerned that "someone who knows something" fill the position and volunteering when no other teachers came forward. Just as the unions in these cases provided one of several avenues for representative decision making, teachers at all three schools understood the role of union representative as one of a number of possible leadership positions; and some teachers moved back and forth between union representative roles and other roles such as department and school council chairships.

Collegial obligation was not confined to a distinct group of teacher leaders, however; other teachers contributed to the collective good by serving as "alternate reps," teaching classes for teachers out of school for negotiating sessions, and intervening when they saw colleagues punished for their involvement in union-related activities. These other contributions suggest both the importance to a broad range of teachers of union-related activities and a more fluid, shared notion of teacher leadership—as sets of tasks that must be done rather than titles or positions—than is commonly recognized in the literature.

Union representatives negotiated relationships among teachers and administrators and between teachers and the union. The social and political status of the individuals who served as union representatives clearly affected the prominence, function, and utility of the union as a source of representation for teachers in school and district decision making. Representatives' involvement in other school leadership capacities, their reputations as teachers, and their professional contacts all contributed to a general understanding of the centrality and legitimacy of the union in the community of teachers.

Rancho's union representatives were current or former department chairs, "learning house" leaders, resource coordinators, and chairs of the School Improvement Council, and were likely to serve in these capacities again. Their authority among teachers seemed simultaneously rooted in individual attributes, their other leadership positions, and in many cases their affiliation with academic departments that were particularly successful in amassing resources. "The union" at Rancho High evoked successful leadership, clout, and a central role in school affairs.

At Onyx Ridge, the sole union representative volunteered for the position primarily out of "a sense of professional obligation" to his Association colleagues. His isolation from other aspects of faculty interaction appeared to contribute to a distance between the Teachers' Association and school activities. Like him, the teacher who "helped him out" felt a personal commitment to the Teachers' Association that predated her tenure at Onyx Ridge. In part by virtue of these two teachers, "the union" did not reflect an integration in school affairs.

At Oak Valley High, after a period of minimal union representation, a new generation of representatives emerged, reflecting a spirit of entrepreneurship and leadership similar to that of Rancho's representatives; they simultaneously served or contemplated serving as department chairships, and held or were working on credentials that provided them with professional options both within and beyond teaching. As the quotation at the beginning of this chapter suggests, the limited and uneven nature of Oak Valley High teachers' opportunities for interaction, as well as the historical relationship in teachers' minds between the union and the union president, made it difficult for many other teachers to utilize union representatives as effectively as they otherwise might have.

THE PERVASIVENESS OF TEACHERS' EXPECTATIONS OF UNIONS

At the end of the 1980s and the beginning of the 1990s, union leaders in Mostaza, Adobe Viejo, and Oak Valley undertook strategies that emphasized more substantive support for teachers' work than ever before. The educational press typically has promoted the notion of a dichotomy between the traditional protection and representation functions elaborated earlier in this chapter and the newer, presumably more "professional" strategies elaborated more fully in the next chapter. Some researchers have envisioned this dichotomy as a sort of trade-off, the question being the conditions under which teachers might be willing to exchange traditional concerns such as security and protection and economic gains, which presumably diminish teaching quality, for more professional items such as expanded opportunities for staff development (McDonnell & Pascal, 1988; Retsinas, 1982). Others have seen these shifts in strategy as an evolutionary "next step," arguing that as relationships between union leaders and administrators become more stable over time, this diminished conflict can somehow be translated into new programs that persuade teachers to assume greater responsibility for the quality of educational programs (Johnson, 1987; Kerchner & Koppich, 1993; Kerchner & Mitchell, 1988).

Teachers in this study persisted in expecting a vigilant union role with respect to matters of job protection, economic issues, and representation—the same general sorts of issues that teachers have expected unions to promote since the inception of these organizations. The commonality of teachers' expectations may have resulted in part from the state policy context that the teachers shared. Within two years of the legalization of collective bargaining in public education in California in 1976, teachers in all three districts selected a bargaining agent; professional organizers from the two state-level organizations who visited the districts may have helped establish common processes and perspectives. Teachers in the three districts also shared a common history of state school finance reforms (some sharply reducing districts' ability to gather local monies) and educational legislation (some constraining teachers' work and others providing new opportunities for teachers' professional diversification and growth), which may have generated consistencies in working conditions that led in turn to similar expectations for union involvement.

Certainly notions about what unions could and should legitimately do was more than a local phenomenon. Like district and state administrators, union leaders in the 1980s and 1990s were increasingly well-read in the educational literature, were well-represented in the educational press, and met routinely with their counterparts across state and national boundaries. As a result of these networks, issues for negotiation and bargaining strategies, including, for example, the idea of collaborative labor relations, were discussed and disseminated across districts (see Bascia, forthcoming).

Any or all of these features—a common blueprint for union strategies at their inception, common state policy effects with which to contend, the ongoing dissemination of ideas among union leaders, and similar evolutionary movement from issue to issue—may have contributed to a consistency in union strategies across district lines and to a consistency in teachers' expectations of unions.

The Role of Collective Agreements

To what extent are teachers' common expectations of unions influenced by similarities in the districts' written contracts? Table 7.1 compares the major provisions delineated in Mostaza, Adobe Viejo, and Oak Valley's collective bargaining agreements in effect between 1989 and 1991, the years this study was undertaken.

A cursory examination of the three contracts reveals several obvious differences. The agreements vary in length and in the specificity of the provisions they contain. Mostaza's, at 111 pages, is the longest and its provisions are the most comprehensive and specific. Adobe Viejo's is nearly as long, at 105 pages, and is the only contract that mentions cooperative labor relations and programs jointly sponsored by union and district administration. Oak Valley's contract, at 42 half-sized pages, is less than one-fourth the size of Mostaza's and its provisions are the least well-specified. But when the provisions are held up against teachers' accounts of the value and shortcomings of unionism in their own work lives, it becomes apparent that the level of specificity, and the particulars of the provisions, contribute to but do not fully explain either teachers' expectations of unions or the value of unionism for teachers.

Mostaza's contract provides guidelines for teachers' extracurricular responsibilities. It distinguishes teachers' rights according to some categories of subject and student assignment. It includes provisions for teacher involvement in decisions concerning class size, evaluation instruments, and Mentor Teacher selection, and ensures teacher majorities on district committees concerned with curriculum, textbook selection, and setting educational objectives. It provides salary incentives for teachers' professional development activities and protects teachers from punishment for job actions such as strikes. The Mostaza Teachers' Association president characterized the extensive nature of this contract as "progressive," especially with respect to protection of teachers' rights and provisions for teachers' inclusion on district committees. But it was the tenor or constructed meaning of contract provisions, more than familiarity with the exact wording, that contributed to Rancho teachers' understanding of union strength and vigilance; teachers' faith in the union extended beyond the contract to a more general belief that "the Association [is] extremely good on [situations where] it's not really a grievance and it's really not an unfair labor practice, it's almost a justice issue."

Adobe Viejo's contract parallels Mostaza's with respect to the number and specificity of provisions, but the more well-delineated items

TABLE 7.1 Major Contractual Provisions

Major category	Mostaza (Rancho)	Adobe Viejo (Onyx Ridge)	Oak Valley (Oak Valley)
Time period of current contract	7/88–7/90 (2 years) Actually ratified 9/89	7/89–7/92 (3 years)	7/89–7/91 (2 years)
Student: teacher ratio for secondary classes (class size)	31:1. Faculty may vote to reallocate within school, within state maximum	29:1	25:1. Principal, with teacher input, determines "personnel:student ratio: given student learning, fiscal, and equity issues
Hours of employment	Minutes per grade calculation; 5 class periods plus 1 prep period. Specified parent conferences; 50 minutes/ week for supervision	"Instructional minutes; 5 class periods. 40-hour week assignment, to be specified by principal	7-hour days
Teaching assignments	Determined by principal. No more than 3 "preps" (different courses). Additional pay for extracurricular assignments	No provision	No provision
Teacher intra-district transfers	Based on seniority of volunteers	Ethnic balance issues considered; "key" teachers exempted; provisions for magnet schools	"Consistency with district needs"
Safety (including student discipline issues)	Teachers are not required to work in unsafe sites. Elementary schools to receive classroom communication systems. Facilities will be evaluated. District will defend employees if students are hurt	District will maintain build-ings. Site security plans will be developed. Teachers have the authority to suspend students	Teachers will report unsafe conditions and when force is used against student. Teachers have the authority to suspend students

TABLE 7.1 *(continued)*

Major category	Mostaza (Rancho)	Adobe Viejo (Onyx Ridge)	Oak Valley (Oak Valley)
Teacher evaluation	Instruments must be agreed upon by teacher and evaluator. Teacher will be compensated for any coursework as part of remediation plan	Mutually determined objectives based upon pupil progress, instructional techniques, learning environment, non-classroom activities	Based on instructional proficiencies, student performance objectives, teaching responsibilities
Professional accountability	Disciplinary procedures for teachers	No provision	No provision
Rights of exclusive representation	Teachers' Association can use school bulletin boards; no inflammatory information. 2 meetings per month per site. No discriminatory action against involved teachers. President paid half salary by district as "consultant," duties to be agreed upon	Teachers' Association can use school bulletin boards. 2 meetings per month per site. 1 representative and 1 alternative representative per site. Representative may talk with teachers after regular faculty meetings	4 meetings per year per site plus additional contract-related meetings. Principal must agree to meet with a "unit building committee" of up to 5 teachers
Prohibited activities	Teachers' Association will not sanction strikes but teachers will be protected if they do stage job actions	Teachers' Association will not sanction strikes, work slow downs, or walk outs	No provision
Agency fee	District deducts Association membership fee from all teachers' monthly salary; non-members' "service fee" can be sent to approved charities	Agency fee election will be held during this contract period; if it passes, then as in Mostaza	No provision

TABLE 7.1 (*continued*)

Major category	Mostaza (Rancho)	Adobe Viejo (Onyx Ridge)	Oak Valley (Oak Valley)
Salary	$23-43,000 during first year of contract, then $24–46,000. Points for military service, VISTA	$ amount unspecified. 6% increase from previous salary during first year of contract, then state cost of living adjustment (COLA)	$26–47,000 during first year of contract, then state cost of living adjustment (COLA)
Health benefits	Up to $3,958; option of 2 plans	Up to amount for least expensive of 3 plan options	Up to $2,537; option of 2 plans
Fringe benefits	No provision	No provision	Teachers may have deductions from salary to TSA
Consulting procedures	Teachers' Association nominates teacher members to district committees such as curriculum, textbook selection, educational objec-tives. All district committees are 50% + 1 teacher	No provision	No provision
Mentor teacher program	Teachers' Association nominates teachers; all teachers at that level (e.g., secondary) vote. Mentors provide staff development, assist new teachers	Teachers apply and district committee (including other teachers) makes selection. Mentors provide "direct services to other teachers"	No provision
Professional incentives	Teachers may move up salary scale if they attend classes, workshops, institutes, or work on special projects	No provision	No provision

TABLE 7.1 (continued)

Major category	Mostaza (Rancho)	Adobe Viejo (Onyx Ridge)	Oak Valley (Oak Valley)
Categories of teachers and others for whom special contractual provisions apply	Nurses, counselors, bilingual, preschool, music, special education teachers	Counselors, bilingual teachers, teachers in year-round schools	No provision
Restructuring	No provisions	"We agree to explore . . . local staffs may be encouraged to consider . . . recognize that it may require waiving contract provisions"	No provision
Contract oversight group	No provisions	Established and scope of issues and duties laid out	No provision

reflect issues and situations not particularly salient to or appropriate for Onyx Ridge teachers. For example, some of the most well-specified items concern teacher transfer provisions, and magnet and year-round school staffing considerations—irrelevant in a school where the principal could and did "pull strings" to attract and retain particular teachers. Similarly irrelevant, or potentially untenable, are provisions that encouraged schools' experimentation with various restructuring reforms, established the Contract Oversight Group, and agreed to an "agency fee" election to determine whether all teachers would be required to pay Teachers' Association dues. While the Mostaza's Teachers' Association historically bargained for provisions that recognized the diversity of teachers' roles and the specificity of their practical needs, the Adobe Viejo Teachers' Association concentrated on provisions that benefited the majority of teachers while ignoring deviations from the norm. Onyx Ridge teachers found the generic occupational classification that drove the AVTA's negotiation strategies inappropriate in philosophical as well as practical terms.

Despite gaps between provisions and the issues of interest to Onyx Ridge teachers, it is possible to infer some relationships between contractual language and working conditions at the school. For example, Adobe Viejo's "hours of employment" provision allowed for site-level discretion over noninstructional time and helped explain why Onyx Ridge teachers understood work allocation as a matter of teacher and principal discretion. Similarly, the provision that excluded union and teacher involvement from mentor teacher selection processes makes it easier to understand why Onyx Ridge teachers considered these positions as autonomous rather than occasions for service to colleagues, as they were in the other two schools in this study.

The Oak Valley contract is particularly unrevealing: Without knowledge of that district's labor history, it would not be possible to infer whether the small number of contract items reflected a low level of conflict between teachers and administrators or masked a series of unresolved issues. The knowledge that historically there was not enough goodwill to negotiate on a broad range of teachers' concerns provides some explanation; so does a former Federation president's comment about the union's tendency to "work hard to get the salary structure up to where it was because it was down so low. So the rights issues went on the side." Many of the kinds of issues specifically delineated in Mostaza and Adobe Viejo contracts were left to administrative discretion in Oak Valley. For example, where class size limits could be altered by faculty vote in Mostaza, in Oak Valley it was principals who determined class size "in consultation" with teachers. There is no provision for assigning teachers to or compensating them for extracurricular activities, a state of affairs with which Oak Valley High teachers were clearly unhappy. With no contractually specified incentives for professional development activities such as the salary increases available to Mostaza teachers, Oak Valley teachers were rewarded more selectively, by administrative recognition.

For all their emerging significance for teachers' legal rights and responsibilities, there was no mention in the written contract of Oak Valley's new program for supporting and evaluating new teachers or the Federation's increased involvement in district decision making. These omissions were partially a result of the timing of the last contract negotiations relative to later developments, but they also reflected the superintendent's reluctance to put these new understandings in writing. The limited nature of Oak Valley's contract also reflected the local importance of personality to authority relations between teachers and administrators.

The relationship between contract provisions and other features of teachers' work is both reciprocal and incomplete. To some extent, teachers' concerns influence what issues unions bargain for and the resulting extensiveness and nature of contract provisions. As Table 7.1 suggests, contract provisions broadly reflect the categories of teachers' expectations that the union ensure job protection, address economic and material concerns, and serve as a form of representation. A more refined level of analysis, however, reveals gaps between contract specifications and teachers' expressed concerns. Some of these gaps reflect the contributions of organizational, fiscal, and political dynamics to the tenor and substance of collective bargaining. Other gaps seem to correspond to differences in the priorities and perspectives of union leaders at the district level and teachers working in the contexts of particular school sites. Teachers' comments suggest that they took exception to what was not in the contract at least as often as they did to what was.

One way to view the gaps between contractual provisions and teachers' concerns is to consider that teachers were more concerned with issues the union had yet to negotiate successfully—class size for Onyx Ridge teachers, for example, or school transfer provisions in Oak Valley. Issues may take time to find their way into the formal collective bargaining process, and they may never be permitted to take root in the written agreement. In this sense, the contract can be considered an historical artifact, an imperfect record of earlier issues and decisions. Few teachers were well-versed in the specifications of contract provisions; instead, the formal contract was only one factor contributing to teachers' perceptions of union effectiveness and only one influence on the nature of teachers' work. The leadership styles of union leaders and administrators, and the impact of their decisions, contributed to a "living contract," providing evidence of where the union had successfully addressed teachers' concerns and suggesting areas where teachers might welcome union intervention.

The practical implications of these points are twofold. First, like educational policy of any type, contract provisions in and of themselves are not likely to change the broad parameters of teachers' work or the dynamics between teachers and others without accompanying shifts in understanding about the nature of teachers' work and teachers' involvement in educational decision making. A second, related implication is that contractual provisions will not necessarily have predictable or uniform effects across school contexts. While contract provisions can contribute powerfully to the structures and relationships inherent to teachers' work lives, these effects occur in the context of a variety of other formal and informal policies and practices that confound and compound the contract's power to influence.

The Greater Decision-Making Environment

The collective bargaining agreement, like relationships among teachers, union, and administrators, does not exist in a vacuum. School board members, parents and other community members, and state agencies and policy-making groups outside the teaching occupation exert influence over important decisions that affect teachers' work (Darling-Hammond & Berry, 1988; Fuhrman, Clune, & Elmore, 1988; Fullan, 1991; McDonnell & Pascal, 1988; McLaughlin, 1990). Recurring funding cycles and electoral politics mean that educational resources are fluid and that policy decisions are made, revoked, and remade (McDonnell & Pascal, 1988; Retsinas, 1982; Russo, 1979). A growing number of corporate, philanthropic, academic, and other "reform partners" increasingly influence the shape of school programs (Bascia, forthcoming). There is much about the political structure of the broader educational institution that limits the extent to which teachers can exercise authority over their work within the contexts of school and district.

Not only are many decisions that affect teaching and learning practices made in a larger and more complex political system, but teachers work within hierarchical and bureaucratized organizations, structures that by their very nature may conflict with teachers' capacities to carry out their work and may serve to sustain conflict between teachers and others (see Bruckerhoff, 1991; Carlson, 1992; Lortie, 1975; Malloy, 1987; Ozga & Lawn, 1981; Sarason,1990; Swanson, 1987; Van Maanen & Barley, 1984). In these settings, the achievement of equilibrium with respect to authority over teachers' work seems unlikely. On the other hand, teachers' need for unions in general and for intervention with respect to specific, recurring issues seems likely. This perspective on teacher unionism as a "logical" response to organizational conditions is a recurring theme in the literature (Apple, 1986; Johnson, 1983; Larson, 1977; Ozga & Lawn, 1981).

The variation in composition and focus of teachers' professional communities, the limited scope of issues unions have been able to address, and unions' subordinate role in organizational terms have meant that unions' capacity to serve as major vehicles for teacher representation has been restricted, at least in their traditional roles. At the same time, these cases attest to teachers' beliefs in the necessity of union presence, at least as an assurance of occupational vigilance. Even teachers who took exception to union strategies or perceived no need for a union "here" or "now" articulated this need, at least in the abstract, at least in the context of other schools, or in other times. Singly or in groups, whether strong union contributors or nonmembers, teachers contacted a union representative when they perceived that a decision made by someone else interfered with their ability to work in accordance with their conceptions of good practice. For teachers in this study, the meaning of "union" is primarily pragmatic rather than ideational, and is rooted in teachers' encounters with particular conditions of their work rather than in abstract notions of professional control or class conflict.

Attention to the occasions when teachers call upon unions for protection and representation yields what might be considered underlying logics or philosophies about teaching within the organizational contexts of schooling (see also Carlson, 1992). Much is revealed about teachers' conceptions of task and expectations of support from others. When teachers ask the union to place or enforce limits on the kinds or amount of work they are expected to do, for example, they articulate what they consider to be the parameters of appropriate work load and assignment.

Union leaders or others who discount as "unprofessional" teachers' calls for union intervention with respect to traditional protection and representation issues are likely to alienate rather than inspire teachers. Because they fail to take into account the real and varied nature of teachers' work and needs for support, such perspectives cannot successfully generate strategies for improving the quality of teaching.

Chapter 8

The New Unions: Representing Teachers' Best Interests

It's really strange to see us turning around and heading [back to shared decision making] given what we've been through. And you see all these national publications coming out and everything, saying where we should be, and we were there.
—Rancho Teachers' Association representative

I don't sense that there's a feeling [among Onyx Ridge teachers] that we need this restructuring.
—Onyx Ridge Teachers' Association representative

This nonadversarial bargaining that they've started, which I'm sure you've heard about, is wonderful. And if that continues, for whatever [the superintendent's] reasons are, who cares, as long as he is willing to negotiate and we can stop all this silly hassling and picketing and not having a contract until April, which was just garbage.
—Oak Valley union representative

During the late 1980s and early 1990s, the period covered by this study, the districts where Rancho, Onyx Ridge, and Oak Valley High Schools are located underwent profound changes in labor–management relations. In each case, union and district leadership developed more extensive and cooperative working relationships. They negotiated collective bargaining agreements with less contention than in the past, structured opportunities for discourse outside the collective bargaining arena, and attempted to expand support for teaching and teachers. There were changes in each case in the issues with which the union was formally concerned, the union's relative position in district life, and teachers' access to union and district decision making.

Previous chapters demonstrated how teachers' evaluations of union strategies are consonant with the issues and interests inherent to their professional communities and their practical needs for protection, support, and representation. This chapter presents teachers' assessments of the value of the shifts in labor relations and union strategies from adversarial and traditional to cooperative and "professional." From these assessments emerge a set of recommendations for teachers' organizations interested in supporting productive forms of teachers' professional communities.

THE LOGIC OF COLLABORATIVE LABOR RELATIONS: SOMETHING FOR EVERYONE

The educational press typically correlates union presence with labor conflict. Toledo's Intern-Intervention Program, a jointly sponsored assistance program for new teachers begun in 1981, may have been the first nationally prominent example of labor–management collaboration (Rauth, 1990), but teacher union and district leadership in a number of districts across the United States have interacted with minimal antipathy for years (Kerchner & Mitchell, 1986; Johnson, 1983, 1984; Lieberman & Bascia, 1990). Kerchner and Caufman (1993) estimate that collaborative labor relations have been attempted in several hundred school districts across the United States. In the mid-1980s, teacher union scholars Charles Kerchner and Douglas Mitchell proposed an intervention strategy for improving the tenor of labor relations through the development of local "educational policy trust agreements" (Bascia, 1991; Kerchner & Koppich, 1993; Kerchner & Mitchell, 1986, 1988). Many organizations at a variety of levels actively encouraged a move away from conflictual relations. Albert Shanker, president of the American Federation of Teachers, made cooperative labor relations a consistent message of his syndicated newspaper column. Foundations and state agencies provided support for various intervention strategies such as conflict resolution training for bargaining teams.

The logic of collaborative labor relations was consistent with the politics of the broader educational restructuring movement in the United States, with which it was frequently affiliated. Indeed, teacher unions were often at the center of the coalitions that sponsored a variety of state and national as well as local educational change efforts—for everything from the curricular integration of educational technology to professional practice schools to teachers' assumption of responsibility for curricular development at the school level. The idea of collaborative labor relations was based on the premise that organizations with an interest in education that may never have worked together—that may even have been political adversaries—could form alliances to support educational initiatives that furthered their mutual interests (Kerchner & Mitchell, 1988; Rosow & Zager, 1989; Shedd & Bacharach, 1991). Because of their political nature and the perception that the standardized bargaining structures of the past had been largely destructive to the quality of educational delivery, cooperative labor relations, like other components of the restructuring movement, were understood to require a sensitivity to context: Both the structures and the particular issues with which they were concerned were to be locally determined.

Union leaders in Mostaza, Adobe Viejo, and Oak Valley found these ideas attractive because they were consonant with their interests in increasing and legitimating their own and teachers' decision-making involvement. "I've never wavered," asserted the former Oak Valley Federation president who coordinated the cooperatively endorsed project. "I want to strengthen the influence of teachers on their daily work life." At about the same time, district administrators realized that their own desires for educational change could not be actualized without significant changes in labor–management dynamics. In some instances the substance of teacher–administrator relations had been almost exclusively and cripplingly conflictual. In other situations, union and district were interested in increasing "public confidence" in education and in teachers themselves (Kerchner & Caufman, 1993). Collaborative labor relations seemed to offer "something for everyone," an opportunity for educators of all stripes and at all levels to enact their visions of educational improvement. As we shall see, however, fulfilling these promises has been a more difficult undertaking than union and administrative leaders imagined.

The relationship between the vitality of the educational enterprise and labor–management relations was most obvious in Mostaza. The previous superintendent had proposed win–win negotiating training for union and district collective bargaining teams several years earlier, but the union had not been receptive: "[We figured] out that win–win means 'You do as I say,'" recounted the Teachers' Association president. When the new superintendent came into office, he found "the tension awful, kids were involved, manipulated, conditions were unsafe, the effects were overwhelming. . . . [I felt that even if there weren't a strike], if the atmosphere didn't change it would be hopeless." As they signed a new contract in September 1989, the Teachers' Association and the new superintendent agreed to participate in win–win negotiation training. Groups of administrators, school board members, and Teachers' Association officials spent

> ... five intensive days [going from] simple to more complex simulations. We started identifying our interests and what we thought the district's interests were going to be. They were going through exactly the same exercise. And then we saw what each other's interests were, and discussed how we could start putting those together as a first step toward the bargaining of a new agreement as well as a new way of working with each other. In the process ... we had a real catharsis. It really finally cleared the air.

Adobe Viejo union and district leadership, too, formally committed themselves to a cooperative relationship with the signing of their contract in 1989. While labor relations had never been particularly cordial, the degree of conflict was much lower than that in Mostaza or Oak Valley. Both sides were interested in increasing the district's momentum in establishing new programs for Adobe Viejo's growing educationally disadvantaged population. While Onyx Ridge's principal perceived the union as having "jumped on the bandwagon" of the superintendent's restructuring efforts, the Teachers' Association president recognized an opportunity to advance the types of innovative, student-centered programs to which he had been committed as a classroom teacher.

In 1987 Oak Valley district leadership agreed to join a state-wide program in collaborative labor relations because they saw an opportunity to add another new program to the district's arsenal of innovations—in this case to address new teachers' practical needs for assistance. For the union, according to the Federation president,

> It was a question of what we could do to reduce the likelihood of first-year teachers being arbitrarily dismissed from the district in view of the fact that they have no legal rights. Foremost in our minds as we developed this program was that it would move that process into a more objective format and would give the union an opportunity to participate in those decisions.

The ensuing shift in labor relations was seen as "a side benefit. ... [In the process of working together on the program], we began forming different perceptions of each other."

LEADERSHIP, POLICIES, PROGRAMS,
AND PRACTICES

The organizational alliances greatly increased interaction among district and union leaders, new district leadership groups, and new district initiatives. In Mostaza and Adobe Viejo, the affiliations between union presidents and superintendents were conspicuous. The leaders attended meetings together, maintained routine phone contact, relied on each other's advice, and kept each other apprised of potential friction points. In Oak Valley, frequent contact among the union president and other officials, district administrators, and collaborative project coordinators engendered a well-developed network of district-level staff. In each district, the committee that coordinated or advised the joint labor-management efforts included teachers and union officials as well as traditional district power wielders, in effect instituting a new tier of leadership with far-ranging influence.

Mostaza initiated a Contract Oversight Group to address minor contractual issues between formal negotiation sessions. A review of the group's first-year activities suggests that much of their attention was focused on articulating a sense of common purpose. Issues that had been sources of contention in the past were handled in new ways. For example, in exchange for the Teachers' Association's agreement to no longer automatically defend teachers who received unsatisfactory performance evaluations, district administration put the onus on principals to provide better support and remediation for such teachers. This committee presented a united front to the rest of the district, providing, for example, a single information session on the new contract for union representatives and principals. The Oversight Group also heard teachers' concerns and tried to resolve issues before they became formal grievances. At the end of their first year, district administration and union leadership discussed providing win–win training for teachers and administrators at the school level.

While eschewing the virtues of collaboration, however, this group did not shift its focus far from traditional collective bargaining issues. For example, while it actively encouraged the formation of special interest caucuses of bilingual, special education, and kindergarten teachers, these groups were intended to identify bargaining issues and develop proposals for instructional resources, not necessarily to take on extensive identities and activities of their own. And while the Oversight Group issued statements of general support for teachers' increased participation in decision making, it made a slow start, endorsing shared decision-making "pilot programs" at only one or two district schools.

In Adobe Viejo, the Contract Oversight Group, "a place to discuss, not negotiate, to propose, to define," met monthly to consider elaborations on traditional bargaining issues such as preparation time for elementary teachers and increasing Teachers' Association representation on traditionally all-administrator district committees. Another of this group's primary functions was to discuss how labor relations could support such school and district innovations as year-round schooling, interdisciplinary instruction, a professional practice school, and shared decision-making structures.

The comparable oversight committee in Oak Valley coordinated and supported the jointly sponsored new teacher assistance program. This group had the legal authority to approve recommendations for advancement or dismissal of probationary teachers, but its influence did not stop there. Discussions between administrator and teacher members evolved into a sophisticated and commonly shared position on "what we expect from our teachers." As in Mostaza, this committee served to forge a common vision among district leaders, with far-ranging implications for supporting a particular conception of teaching. Where Adobe Viejo's Oversight Group tended to delegate program administration to other district committees, Oak Valley's small administrator pool meant a more responsive structure; as a result, group deliberations led quickly to improvements in working relations, changes in resource allocations, and new district procedures. The union president now felt entitled to travel to school sites and meet with principals around a variety of issues. The oversight group supported the emergence of new professional development opportunities, such as an ongoing mentoring group for second- and third-year teachers. Finally, a cadre of teacher leaders emerged from this group, whose advice was considered and involvement sought in other innovative program areas across the district.

The highly visible new teacher assistance program released a handful of veteran teachers from their own classrooms to observe, provide resources and informal feedback, demonstrate lessons, advocate with administrators, and otherwise assist first-year teachers in all the district's schools. These "consultants" also conducted the formal evaluations that ultimately resulted in new teachers' continued employment or dismissal. After working with the consultants, principals reported improvements in their own capacities to support new teachers. New teachers came to take peer coaching and support for granted and, in their second and third years, to expect structured opportunities to improve their classroom practice by working with other teachers. As tenured teachers became aware of the program, they let it be known that they also would welcome peer coaching opportunities. Basking in teachers' general approval of the program, the Federation proposed a plan to have consultants work with tenured teachers who received unsatisfactory evaluations. In exchange for this assistance, the Federation would no longer automatically defend teachers who showed little improvement after such intervention.

As fieldwork for this study came to a close, Oak Valley leadership initiated a second collaborative project to increase teacher involvement in shaping the district's professional development programs. In these ways, the fruits of collaborative labor relations served to change the local culture around and to create support for the improvement of teaching, and the Federation began to articulate its position as a local custodian of professional teaching standards.

NICHES, INCENTIVES, AND MATCHES

Beyond their political impetus and implications, the shifts in union focus detailed above must also be commended as attempts to enhance local support for teaching. Any assessment of the ultimate success of these efforts, however, must move beyond the focus on district-level activities unfortunately so typical of the research on teacher unionism, to inquire about teachers' responses and reactions. When we compare teachers' responses across school sites within the same districts, it is evident that *district-level* policies and practices influence teachers' commitment, sense of efficacy, and professional identity (McLaughlin & Talbert, 1993). At the same time, teachers' daily interactions and *school-level* policies and practices result in differences in teachers' reported job satisfaction, collegiality, learning opportunities, and capacity to incorporate new teaching practices (see, for example, Hargreaves, Davis, Fullan, Wignall, Stager, & Macmillan, 1992; Little, 1982; McLaughlin, 1993; McLaughlin & Yee, 1988; Oakes, 1989; Rosenholz, 1989). The previous chapters described how school and district features each contributed to teachers' conceptions of professional community and created contexts for their practical needs for protection and support. These analyses all point to the "embedded" or multilevel nature of effects of policy on the practice of teaching.

District-level union and administrative leaders across all three case studies were clearly aware of the salience of school context to the success of their efforts. Personnel in each district could identify school faculties that were inspired by the collaboratively sponsored programs to engage more fully and successfully with curriculum, colleagues, and students, and other schools where teachers ignored or rejected the innovations. Some teachers found the new nonadversarial dynamic between union and district administration consonant with their own conceptions of professional community, while others did not find the logic of collaboration persuasive. In some contexts, the new projects had an obvious practical utility, filling a perceived gap in service or support, providing intellectual grist for teachers' professional growth, and creating valued new roles and activities. At other schools, the need for programmatic change was not obvious, and for some teachers the whole enterprise was threatening and debilitating.

Rancho: Loss and Fragmentation

For Rancho teachers, the changes in relations between union and district leadership were highly visible but of questionable value. A year after signing the last contract, union and school board returned to the bargaining table to renegotiate teachers' salaries, each side newly aware of the other's interests and operational constraints. Confronted with a diminished budget but committed to productive negotiations, they "agreed on the goal of getting salaries into the upper quartile while recognizing the necessity for fiscal integrity." The Teachers' Association president believed that "in general, our members are pleased because they are tough enough to do what's right." But not all teachers responded favorably; "a group that would have been our most militant [teachers] . . . always negative, [is] very suspicious of our relationship with the district right now." Some teachers questioned the necessity of a compromise salary settlement when "they knew they could win" a larger increase if they waged a strike, but, according to the union president, "it was important [for the Teachers' Association] not to strike for community relations reasons." For many teachers, most significant was the lack of any appreciable gain in resources for teaching. While the district's mantra of "no money" was only too familiar, teachers were not sure that the union still acted as their advocate. In the face of recurring and chronic shortages of materials and support, Rancho teachers' historical loyalty to the Teachers' Association was seriously strained by the shift in union strategies.

The impact of fiscal adversity on labor relations was more than just a local occurrence. In some ways, the collaborative labor relations phenomenon can be understood as a product of a brief window between economic recessions of the early and later 1980s, when districts were able to settle some of the salary and instructional resource issues more productively than they had in the past, and when it was possible to fund the necessary time, materials, and support staff for the development of new programs. In the year following this study, however, a new recession tightened district budgets and strained relationships among teachers and unions as well as between unions and school boards in many districts, including those attempting cooperative arrangements (see also Kerchner & Koppich, 1993). Where programs are cut or teachers' work is affected by a loss of resources, colleagues, or their own jobs, demoralization and lessened commitment are likely and understandable results. The challenge for union and district leadership is to find ways to capitalize on the potential utility of the new relationships, structures, and programs in fiscally difficult times, to strive for real consensus among members of the district community.

Mostaza teachers might have been more accepting of the Teachers' Association's compromise strategy if they believed the leadership alliance was committed to substantive changes in the quality of their work lives. Especially when compared with Adobe Viejo's emphasis on programs for disadvantaged students or Oak Valley's concern with support for teaching, the lack of programmatic focus in the Mostaza brand of "new unionism" was obvious. The commitment to shared decision making that emerged from the 1989 contract negotiations could have been a rallying point for teachers, but the district showed little evidence of real support for site-based management.

"It's so easy to get caught up in 'They're a bunch of dishonest jerks, I've been through this 25 times,'" said a Rancho English teacher. "Once burned, twice shy. I'm very leery." The charge that the Teachers' Association was "in bed with the district" was a major campaign issue for one candidate in a close contest for the union presidency. A Teachers' Association internal document of the time revealed a concern that "infighting within the Association colors our dealing with management." For Rancho teachers, current events seemed consistent with the kinds of actions that had alienated them in the past. The new alliance had not managed to break down traditional divisions between teachers and administrators, and with the loss of the union as a focus for teachers' collective identification, teachers' professional community began to fragment. Whatever vitality the professional community of teachers once had was seriously threatened.

Onyx Ridge: Mismatch and Indifference

When asked, Onyx Ridge teachers said they generally approved of their Teachers' Association's new position in district life. But the new collaborative relationship between union and administration seemed of little real consequence beyond "being able to say we can teach for 2 or 3 years and not have to worry about job actions." When they considered their own condition—their students, their conceptions of themselves as different from teachers elsewhere in the district—Onyx Ridge teachers viewed the value of the "new unionism" in different terms. The district's proposal that school staffs adopt some form of shared decision making had made its way into the school but found no toehold: With representative decision-making structures in place, teachers saw little value in a shift in authority relations and for all their utility for teachers who taught educationally disadvantaged students, the host of collaboratively sponsored programs available to Adobe Viejo schools was not attractive to Onyx Ridge teachers. Accustomed to finding professional community in individually sought, typically subject-based connections with colleagues throughout the region, teachers were not immediately attracted by the emphasis on school-based change efforts.

Onyx Ridge teachers' indifference was in some ways the result of the minimal attention paid to this school by district leadership. With so many other schools with large populations of disadvantaged students, the relatively privileged Onyx Ridge was not the new alliance's first priority. By accepting the premise that the school had little to offer and little to gain from the new collaborative programs, the union–district alliance relinquished the opportunity to engage with Onyx Ridge teachers. Such premises tend to become self-fulfilling.

Onyx Ridge teachers who had been committed to the Teachers' Association found that the presence of the Contract Oversight Group (COG) made union involvement less satisfying and productive than before. Onyx Ridge's union representative found union meetings less substantive than in the past and was concerned that decisions were being made from a more exclusive base than previously: "The COG doesn't do classroom teachers any good. The leadership is involved, it's a little cliquish . . . [and] they don't work here [in the schools]." The Adobe Viejo case, like Mostaza, exemplifies how unions can focus on the internal dynamics of a new oversight group, to the exclusion of union membership at large. Oversight teams can easily isolate themselves, lose the commitment of their constituencies, and come to function, or appear to be functioning, much like the traditional hierarchical governance structures they were intended to replace. Keeping teacher representatives involved in substantive decision making keeps the organization vital.

Oak Valley: New Strength and Enduring Questions

Of the three cases, Oak Valley's faculty found the greatest utility in the new union–management relationship and collaboratively sponsored programs. A union leader perceived the changes as "a reversal, almost like the tide turning"; for many teachers the overriding perception was one of a new congruence with deeply held beliefs and values. The new teacher assistance project was not visible to as many teachers as it might have been in a smaller, less departmentalized school than Oak Valley High, but teachers approved of its expansion to provide remediation for tenured teachers, because such a plan was consonant with their own professional values. Teachers liked what they perceived as a new "strong moral tone" in the union's new position on teacher protection issues. They valued the collaborative programs and the Federation's newly effective role in a general sense. Unlike in Mostaza and Adobe Viejo, Oak Valley's union–district alliance resulted in greater, not fewer, opportunities for teachers' participation. The collaboratively sponsored programs expanded teachers' involvement in program planning and implementation, areas previously controlled by administrators. The symbolic value of teachers' increased participation in district life should not be underestimated. Oak Valley teachers' professional community had been along lines more consistent with teachers' values, and teacher–administrator divisions diminished in importance.

Even in the Oak Valley case, however, evidence that the new unionism would make a deep or sustained difference in the quality of teachers' work lives was not entirely conclusive. For all of the increases in teachers' contributions to district decision making, there were intimations of the tenuousness of administrators' willingness to include union and teachers in district decision making. "[District administrators] will set aside a power question by saying, 'Well of course we reserve the right to decide, but let's talk about it all together now, in this context,'" said the union president. While other districts have codified new relationships and new programs in contract language, Oak Valley administrators showed reluctance.

A contract's reflection of new understandings about the union's and teachers' new roles in a district does not ensure that power dynamics have been resolved. Even to the extent that local administrators are willing to share authority, the hierarchical nature of school systems is reinforced by larger systemic forces. A new superintendent, a powerful state policy that requires traditional authority relationships for compliance, or any number of other events could threaten the collaborative nature of relationships in Oak Valley. The strength of the traditional power paradigm not only limits teachers' involvement in substantive decision making but may serve to sustain conflict between teachers and others because of differences in understandings about how teachers should carry out their work (Malloy, 1987; Ozga & Lawn, 1981; Swanson,

1987; Van Maanen & Barley, 1984). In such a climate, the achievement of equilibrium with respect to authority relations seems unlikely.

IMPLICATIONS FOR REFORM

Teachers' early responses to the dynamics and programs that emerged from cooperative labor relations suggest that differences in perspective between district and school can have serious consequences for teacher commitment to new forms of unionism, to their schools and districts, and to teaching as an occupation. Union leaders' capacities to extend their attention beyond new relationships with district administration, to pay attention to teachers' perspectives and respond to their needs, determine the utility teachers will find in the strategies with which unions are concerned, however traditional or innovative their nature.

Building on Existing Professional Communities

The cases in this study suggest that the viability of union strategies in teachers' professional lives depends on union recognition of and respect for teachers' professional communities as they are constructed by teachers at the school level: that union strategies capitalize on teachers' patterns of interaction, the issues around which teachers find their commonality, and teachers' sources of inspiration and support. These values and relationships are the effective points for engaging and supporting teachers. Strategies appropriate in one setting will not necessarily be attractive or useful for teachers in another because of local differences in conceptions of teaching and needs for support.

For example, the Mostaza Teachers' Association might engage Rancho teachers by providing training for and honoring the decisions that emerge from school- and district-based shared decision-making structures. Onyx Ridge teachers would be more attracted to voluntary content- or curriculum-based projects that appealed to and extended their essentially academic subject-based orientations. Projects with explicit "moral" as well as practical bases that extend teachers' connections across department, school, and district boundaries are likely to be most successful in engaging Oak Valley teachers. While these particular prescriptions might be applied to other school contexts, the more general points are that teachers' professional communities take many forms and that reform strategies should follow analyses of the interactions and focuses of greatest concern to teachers in particular school contexts.

Programs of Meaningful Substance

The enhancement and expansion of teachers' professional communities also depends on the provision of a practical focus. Rancho teachers would value shared decision making at school and district levels that emphasized programmatic as well as resource-related issues and resulted in improvements in teachers' interactions with students. Onyx Ridge teachers might be attracted by educational programs that are framed in ways that emphasize their benefits to the broad range of Onyx Ridge students, from the gifted to those who are "falling through the cracks." The Onyx Ridge case demonstrates how engaging teachers in educational reforms across diverse school contexts may require a variety of programmatic options, or options whose versatility is made explicit. Oak Valley's peer assistance and teacher-initiated staff development programs were attractive to teachers because they filled obvious needs for professional development and increased opportunities for collegial interaction.

Programs of meaningful substance have the potential to enhance and extend the local professional community and signal a union's commitment to teachers' practical needs. The importance of repeated and consistent evidence that a union honors its commitment to teachers cannot be overestimated. As unions move into new partnerships with administrators and others, their ongoing commitment to teachers must be demonstrated in ways that acknowledge and are logically consistent with teachers' historical needs for protection and representation. Rancho teachers would be convinced by evidence of the Teachers' Association commitment to finding creative ways to finance instructional resources. The Adobe Viejo Teachers' Association could negotiate special resource, scheduling, and status provisions that reflected Onyx Ridge teachers' particular conceptions of their professional roles. The Oak Valley Federation enhanced its position with teachers when it took up, and successfully championed, teachers' rights issues in ways that did not result in antagonism between teachers and administrators.

Strengthening Teacher Commitment
to School and District Life

Unions must work to ensure that teacher involvement in and commitment to the broader substance of school and district life increase rather than diminish by virtue of the new structures and programs. New representative forums such as district-level oversight groups can limit teachers' traditional access to union decision making and must be carefully monitored. The substantive programs also must be assessed for their capacity to increase teachers' involvement and commitment. Union viability depends on ensuring that opportunities for teacher involvement are meaningful—that they concern issues relevant to teachers' work lives and provide teachers with an effective vehicle for contributing to decisions that affect their practice.

The Mostaza and Oak Valley cases demonstrate that the new relationships do not seriously challenge authority relations between teachers and administrators, but leave in place many of the structures that reinforce teachers' subordination (see Kerchner & Caufman, 1993). Under such conditions, how successful can unions be at transforming their own roles as teachers' professional organizations? To the extent that administrators are unable or unwilling to share power with teachers, the old dynamics will remain in place and teachers' traditional concerns will continue to be salient.

The cases in this study suggest how readily unions, like any other form of teacher representation, can lose their utility for teachers. In such circumstances, teachers will lose interest in what is potentially an important source of collective identity and a means for improving the quality of their work lives. Such estrangement becomes reciprocal: Teachers alienated from their local forum for legal representation contribute less to the formation of issues and strategies with which unions are concerned, and in exchange discover that union strategies are increasingly inappropriate in relation to their professional needs and values.

While other forms of teacher affiliation—departmental collaborations within schools, subject area and special interest networks that span school and district boundaries, and so on—can be productive arenas for professional interaction, unions represent important and unique structures for teachers' construction of practice, across disciplinary divisions, in locally appropriate ways. Teachers' active involvement in educational activities beyond their own classrooms means their greater influence in the quality of their working relationships with students and colleagues. To the extent that unions successfully engage teachers' interest and involvement—not only in union-sponsored activities but in school and district life more generally—teachers stand to gain more effective and responsive means of assuming authority over their practice, in both the short and the long run.

Appendix: Characteristics of Study Respondents

All individuals who are quoted in the study are listed below (Table A.1). All identification numbers refer to the cataloguing system used by the Center for Research on the Context of Secondary School Teaching (CRC). Some respondents were specifically interviewed for this study; they are listed in the far right column as UNION interviews. Others were interviewed for other purposes by this and other researchers. Many more interviews were analyzed for the study than appear in this appendix, but these respondents' comments are included in the study because of the clarity of their explanations or because they are representative of comments made by a number of other respondents. This appendix demonstrates the diversity of teacher and administrator perspectives that contributed to the construction of each case study.

Identification numbers that begin with "OR" are Onyx Ridge teachers and administrators; "OV" refers to Oak Valley, and "RA" to Rancho. "XX" identification numbers belong to district-level (including union) officials in the Oak Valley district, while "YY" refers to Adobe Viejo, and "ZZ" to Mostaza personnel. "CRC core" refers to open-ended, exploratory interviews conducted by CRC researchers during 1988–89 and 1989–90. "DEPT" refers to interviews conducted in 1989–90 for a study of the practical and social functions of academic departments in these schools (see Siskin, 1994). "TFU" interviews, in 1989–90, followed classroom observations and focused on how teachers think about relationships between subject matter content and their students in these schools (see Cohen, McLaughlin, & Talbert, 1993; Stodolsky, in press). "STUDENT" interviews, also conducted in 1989–90, emphasized teachers' perceptions of particular student groups within these schools (see Phelan & Davidson, 1993; Phelan, Davidson, & Cao, forthcoming).

TABLE A.1 Profiles of Individuals Quoted in this Study

ID#	Gender	Dept.	Years in school/ in dist.	Special roles(s)	Interview type(s)
OR008	F	math	8/23	alternate union rep	union
OR009	M	science	9/21	—	CRC core
OR010	M	social studies	4/14	student body officer coordinator	union
OR014	M	science	5/20	—	CRC core
OR015	F	social studies	6/20	department chair	CRC core
OR016	F	math	9/19	department chair, coach	CRC core, union
OR017	F	math, foreign lang.	3/6	—	CRC core
OR018	F	social studies	4/22	—	CRC core, union
OR025	M	math	10/20	coach	CRC core
OR033	F	foreign language	9/13	department chair	CRC core
OR044	F	foreign language	6/10	—	union
OR045	F	English	1/21	—	CRC core
OR047	M	science	8/27	former union pres., union rep	CRC core, union
OR051	F	English	4/10	coach	CRC core, TFU
OR052	F	math	8/14	coach	union
OR056	F	—	—	head counselor	CRC core
OR057	F	—	—	principal	CRC core, union
OV006	F	science	7/8	senior union rep	union
OV008	F	social studies	18/18	faculty advisory rep	CRC core, dept.
OV014	F	foreign language	7/7	department chair	union
OV027	M	science	28/28	—	union

TABLE A.1 *(continued)*

ID#	Gender	Dept.	Years in school/ in dist.	Special roles(s)	Interview type(s)
OV031	F	special education	3/5	union rep	union
OV046	M	industrial arts	28/28	department chair	CRC core
OV056	F	English	13/13	former union rep	union
OV059	M	industrial arts	16/16	Colloquium rep	union
OV067	F	home economics	17/17	department chair, faculty advisory rep	union
OV105	M	industrial arts	19/20	former union pres.	union
OV106	M	English	5/7	—	CRC core
OV112	F	special education	12/12	department chair, union rep	union
OV130	F	math	13/18	union rep	union
OV136	M	—	—	former principal, associate supt.	CRC core, CPRE
OV139	M	—	—	assistant principal	CRC core
OV140	M	—	—	student leadership coordinator	union
OV155	M	—	1/1	principal	CRC core, union
RA003	F	English	14/20	—	CRC core, union
RA016	F	physical education	2/9	—	CRC core
RA021	M	science	14/23	senior union rep, school council chair	CRC core, union
RA027	M	industrial arts	14/23	department chair	CRC core
RA029	F	English	13/20	department chair, former school council chair	CRC core student, union
RA033	M	art	14/20	department chair, union rep	CRC core, union

TABLE A.1 (*continued*)

ID#	Gender	Dept.	Years in school/ in dist.	Special roles(s)	Interview type(s)
RA035	F	math	7/17	—	TFU
RA038	F	English	10/13	—	union
RA039	M	social studies	7/19	department chair	CRC core
RA058	M	industrial arts	10/19	—	union
RA065	M	science	4/4	former alternative union rep, learning house leader	union
RA070	F	English	13/17	—	CRC core
RA071	M	social studies	4/20	—	CRC core
RA081	M	—	—	former principal	CRC core
RA087	M	—	—	principal	CRC core, union
SC001	M	social studies	—	former Rancho teacher and union rep	union
XX002	M	—	—	union president	union
XX004	M	—	—	former union president	union
YY011	M	—	—	union president	union
ZZ001	F	—	—	former sup't.	union
ZZ003	M	—	—	superintendent	CRC core, union
ZZ019	M	—	—	union president	union

References

American Educator. (1987, Spring). Shared decision making at the school site: Moving towards a professional model: An interview with Patrick O'Rourke, pp. 10–17, 46.

Apple, M. (1986). *Teachers and texts: A political economy of class and gender relations in education.* New York: Routledge & Kegan Paul.

Bacharach, S. B., & Mitchell, S. M. (1981). Interest group politics in school districts: The case of local teachers' unions. In S. B. Bacharach (Ed.), *Organizational behavior in schools and school districts* (pp. 495–526). New York: Praeger.

Bascia, N. (1991, April). The trust agreement projects: Establishing local professional cultures for teachers. Paper presented at the American Educational Research Association annual meeting, Chicago.

Bascia, N. (forthcoming). Caught in the crossfire: Restructuring, collaboration, and the "problem school." In A. Hargreaves & S. Lawton (Eds.), *The realities of restructuring.*

Braun, R. J. (1972). *Teachers and power: The story of the American Federation of Teachers.* New York: Simon & Schuster.

Bruckerhoff, C. E. (1991). *Between classes: Faculty life at Truman High.* New York: Teachers College Press.

Carlson, D. (1992). *Teachers and crisis: Urban school reform and teachers' work culture.* New York: Routledge, Chapman and Hall.

Carter, B. (1991, April). The Stanford/Schools Collaborative: Building an inquiring community of practitioners and researchers. Paper presented at the American Educational Research Association annual meeting, Chicago.

Casner-Lotto, J. (1988). Expanding the teacher's role: Hammond's school improvement process. *Phi Delta Kappan, 69*(5), 349–353.

Clune, W. H. (1990). Research from three views of curriculum policy in the school context: The school as policy mediator, policy critic, and policy constructor. In M. W. McLaughlin, J. E. Talbert, & N. Bascia (Eds.), *The context of teaching in secondary schools: Teachers' realities* (pp. 256–270). New York: Teachers College Press.

Cohen, D. K., McLaughlin, M. W., & Talbert, J. E. (Eds.). (1993). *Teaching for understanding: Challenges for policy and practice.* San Francisco: Jossey-Bass.

Cole, S. (1968). The unionization of teachers: Determinants of rank-and-file support. *Sociology of Education, 41,* 37–66.

Corwin, R. G. (1970). *Militant professionalism: A study of organizational conflict in high schools.* New York: Appleton-Century-Crofts.

CRC. (1989). *Continuation application for years 3–5* (Vol. 1) (Tech. doc.). Stanford, CA: Center for Research on the Context of Secondary School Teaching.

Darling-Hammond, L., & Berry, B. (1988). *The evolution of teacher policy.* Washington, DC: RAND Corporation.

David, J. L. (1989). *Restructuring in progress: Lessons from pioneering districts.* Washington, DC: National Governors Association Center for Policy Research.

Densmore, K. (1987). Book reviews. *Educational Studies, 18*(3), 453–463.

Elmore, R. (1989). *Early experiences in restructured schools: Voices from the field.* Washington, DC: National Governors Association Center for Policy Research.

Englert, R. M. (1979). Collective bargaining in public education: Conflict and its context. *Education and Urban Society, 11*(2), 255–269.

Fleishman, J. (1988). The effects of decision framing and others' behavior on cooperation in a social dilemma. *Journal of Conflict Resolution, 32,* 162–180.

Freedman, S. (1987). Who will care for our children? Removing nurturance from the teaching profession: Three teachers' views of the Carnegie Report. *Democratic Schools, 3*(1), 7, 15.

Fuhrman, S., Clune, W., & Elmore, R. (1988). Research on education reform: Lessons on the implementation of policy. *Teachers College Record, 90*(2), 237–258.

Fullan, M., with Stiegelbauer, S. (1991). *The new meaning of educational change.* New York: Teachers College Press.

Glaser, B., & Strauss, A. (1967). *The discovery of grounded theory: Strategies for qualitative research.* Chicago: Aldine.

Haberman, M. (1986). Licensing teachers: Lessons from other professions. *Phi Delta Kappan, 67*(10), 719–722.

Hargreaves, A. (1993). Individualism and individuality: Reinterpreting the teacher culture. In J. W. Little & M. W. McLaughlin (Eds.), *Teachers' work: Individuals, colleagues, and contexts* (pp. 51–76). New York: Teachers College Press.

Hargreaves, A., Davis, J., Fullan, M., Wignall, R., Stager, M., & Macmillan, R. (1992). *Secondary school work cultures and educational change.* Toronto: Ontario Institute for Studies in Education.

Heckathorn, D. (1988). Collective sanctions and the creation of prisoner's dilemma norms. *American Journal of Sociology, 94,* 535–562.

Huberman, M. (1991). The professional life cycle of teachers. *Teachers College Record, 91*(3), 31–57.

Huberman, M. (1993). The model of the independent artisan in teachers' professional relations. In J. W. Little & M. W. McLaughlin (Eds.), *Teachers' work: Individuals, colleagues, and contexts* (pp. 11–50). New York: Teachers College Press.

Johnson, S. M. (1983). Teacher unions in schools: Authority and accommodation. *Harvard Educational Review, 53*(3), 309–326.

Johnson, S. M. (1984). *Teacher unions in schools*. Philadelphia: Temple University Press.

Johnson, S. M. (1987). Can schools be reformed at the bargaining table? *Teachers College Record, 89*(2), 269–280.

Johnson, S. M. (1988). Pursuing professional reform in Cincinnati. *Phi Delta Kappan, 69*(10), 746–751.

Johnson, S. M. (1990). The primacy and potential of high school departments. In M. W. McLaughlin, J. E. Talbert, & N. Bascia (Eds.), *The context of teaching in secondary schools: Teachers' realities* (pp. 167–184). New York: Teachers College Press.

Kerchner, C. T., & Caufman, K. D. (1993). Building the airplane while it's rolling down the runway. In C. T. Kerchner & J. E. Koppich (Eds.), *A union of professionals: Labor relations and educational reform* (pp. 1–24). New York: Teachers College Press.

Kerchner, C. T., & Koppich, J. E. (1993). *A union of professionals: Labor relations and educational reform*. New York: Teachers College Press.

Kerchner, C. T., & Mitchell, D. E. (1986). Teaching reform and union reform. *Elementary School Journal, 86*(4), 449–470.

Kerchner, C. T., & Mitchell, D. E. (1988). *The changing idea of a teachers' union*. Philadelphia: Falmer Press.

Larson, M. S. (1977). *The rise of professionalism: A sociological analysis*. Berkeley: University of California Press.

Lichtenstein, G., McLaughlin, M. W., & Knudsen, J. (1992). Teacher empowerment and professional knowledge. In A. Lieberman (Ed.), *The Changing Contexts of Teaching*. Chicago: NSSE Yearbook, University of Chicago Press.

Lieberman, A., & Bascia, N. (1990). The trust agreement: A cooperative labor compact (Report for the Stuart Foundations). Berkeley: Policy Analysis for California Education (PACE).

Lieberman, M. (1988). Professional ethics in public education: An autopsy. *Phi Delta Kappan, 70*(2), 159–160.

Little, J. W. (1982). Norms of collegiality and experimentation: Workplace conditions of school success. *American Educational Research Journal, 19*(3), 325–340.

Little, J. W. (1990). The persistence of privacy: Autonomy and initiative in teachers' professional relations. *Teachers College Record, 91*(4), 509–535.

Little, J. W., & Mclaughlin, M. W. (1993). *Teachers' work: Individuals, colleagues, and contexts*. New York: Teachers College Press.

Lortie, D. (1975). *Schoolteacher*. Chicago: University of Chicago Press.

Louis, K. S. (1990). Social and community values and the quality of teacher work life. In M. W. McLaughlin, J. E. Talbert, & N. Bascia (Eds.), *The context of teaching in secondary schools: Teachers' realities* (pp. 17–39). New York: Teachers College Press.

Lowe, W. T. (1965). Who joins which teachers' group? *Teachers College Record, 66*, 614–619.

Malloy, C. (1987, January). The Carnegie Commission Report: A dangerous utopia for teachers. *Radical Teacher*, 23–25.

Marwell, G., & Ames, R. E. (1979). Experiments on the provision of public goods, I: Resources, interest, group size, and the free-rider problem. *American Journal of Sociology, 84*, 1335–1360.

Marwell, G., & Ames, R. E. (1980). Experiments on the provision of public goods, II: Provision points, experience, and the free-rider problem. *American Journal of Sociology, 85*, 926–937.

Marwell, G., & Ames, R. E. (1981). Economists free ride: Does anyone else? Experiments on the provision of public goods, IV. *Journal of Public Economics, 15*, 295–310.

Marwell, G., Oliver, P., & Prahl, R. (1988). Social networks and collective action: A theory of the critical mass, III. *American Journal of Sociology, 94*, 502–534.

Matlock, N. (1987). Building a consensus for change in education: Three teachers' views of the Carnegie Report. *Democratic Schools, 3*(1), 6, 14.

McCaleb, T. S., & Wagner, R. E. (1985). The experimental search for free riders: Some reflections and observations. *Public Choice, 47*, 479–490.

McDonnell, L. (1981). Public control and the power of organized teachers. Unpublished paper. Santa Monica, CA: RAND Corporation.

McDonnell, L. M., & Pascal, A. H. (1988). *Teacher unions and educational reform.* Washington, DC: RAND Corporation.

McLaughlin, M. (1990). The Rand change agent study revisited: Macro perspectives and micro realities. *Educational Researcher, 19*(9), 11–16.

McLaughlin, M. (1993). What matters most in teachers' workplace context? In J. W. Little & M. W. McLaughlin (Eds.), *Teachers' work: Individual, colleagues, and contexts* (pp. 79–103). New York: Teachers College Press.

McLaughlin, M. W., & Talbert, J. E. (1993). *Contexts that matter for teaching and learning: Strategic opportunities for meeting the nation's educational goals.* Stanford, CA: Center for Research on the Context of Secondary School Teaching.

McLaughlin, M. W., & Yee, S. M. (1988). School as a place to have a career. In A. Lieberman (Ed.), *Building a professional culture in schools* (pp. 23–44). New York: Teachers College Press.

Metz, M. H. (1990). How social class differences shape the context of teachers' work. In M. W. McLaughlin, J. E. Talbert, & N. Bascia (Eds.), *The context of teaching in secondary schools: Teachers' realities* (pp. 40–107). New York: Teachers College Press.

Mitchell, D. E., & Kerchner, C. T. (1983). Labor relations and teacher policy. In L. S. Shulman & G. Sykes (Eds.), *Handbook of teaching and policy* (pp. 214–238). New York: Longman.

Oakes, J. (1989). What educational indicators? The case for assessing the school context. *Educational Evaluation and Policy Analysis, 11*(2), 181–199.

Oliver, P. (1980). Rewards and punishments as selective incentives for collective action: Theoretical investigations. *American Journal of Sociology, 85*, 1356–1375.

Oliver, P., & Marwell, G. (1988). The paradox of group size in collective action: A theory of the critical mass, II. *American Sociological Review, 53*, 1–8.

Olson, M. (1965). *The logic of collective action.* Cambridge, MA: Harvard University Press.

Ozga, J., & Lawn, M. (1981). *Teachers, professionalism and class: A study of organized teachers.* London: Falmer Press.

Phelan, P. K., & Davidson, A. L. (Eds.). (1993). *Renegotiating cultural diversity in American schools.* New York: Teachers College Press.

Phelan, P. K., Davidson, A. L., & Cao, H. T. (1993). Students' multiple worlds: Navigating the borders of family, peer, and school cultures. In P. Phelan, & A. L. Davidson (Eds.), *Renegotiating cultural diversity in American schools* (pp. 52–88). New York: Teachers College Press.

Rauth, M. (1990). Exploring heresy in collective bargaining and school restructuring. *Phi Delta Kappan, 71*(10), 781–784.

Retsinas, J. (1982). Teachers: Bargaining for control. *American Educational Research Journal, 19*(3), 353–396.

Rosenholz, S. J. (1989). *Teachers' workplace: The social organization of schools.* New York: Longman Press.

Rosow, J. M., & Zager, R. (1989). *Allies in educational reform.* San Francisco: Jossey-Bass.

Russo, J. B. (1979). Changes in bargaining structures: The implications of the Serrano decision. *Education and Urban Society, 11*(2), 208–218.

Sarason, S. (1990). *The predictable failure of educational reform.* San Francisco: Jossey-Bass.

Shedd, J. B., & Bacharach, S. B. (1991). *Tangled hierarchies: Teachers as professionals and the management of schools.* San Francisco: Jossey-Bass.

Simpkins, E., McCutcheon, A. V., & Alec, R. (1979). Arbitration and policy issues in school contracts. *Education and Urban Society, 11*(2), 241–254.

Siskin, L. S. (1994). *Realms of knowledge: Academic departments in secondary schools.* London: Falmer Press.

Siskin, L. S., & Little, J. W. (Eds.). (1995). *The high school department: Perspectives on the subject organization of secondary schools.* New York: Teachers College Press.

Sizer, T. R. (1984). *Horace's compromise: The dilemma of the American high school.* Boston: Houghton Mifflin.

Smith, H. (1991, April). Foxfire-affiliated teacher networks. Paper presented at the American Educational Research Association annual meeting, Chicago.

Smith, V. (1980). An experimental comparison of three public good decision mechanisms. *Scandinavian Journal of Economics, 81,* 198–215.

Stodolsky, S. S. (1988). *The subject matters: Classroom activity in mathematics and social studies.* Chicago: University of Chicago Press.

Stodolsky, S. S. (in press). A framework for subject matter comparisons in high schools. *Teaching and Teacher Education.*

Swanson, E. (1987). A teacher's view of the Carnegie blueprint: Three teachers' views of the Carnegie Report. *Democratic Schools, 3*(1), 4–5, 13.

Sweeney, J. (1973). An experimental investigation of the free-rider problem. *Social Science Research, 2,* 277–292.

Sykes, G. (1986). The social consequences of standard-setting in the professions.

Paper prepared for the Task Force on Teaching as a Profession, Carnegie Forum on Education and the Economy.

Sykes, G. (1987). Reckoning with the spectre. *Educational Researcher, 16*(6), 19–21.

Talbert, J. E. (1991, April). Teacher track as a locus of professional community. Paper presented to the American Educational Research Association annual meeting, Chicago.

Tyack, D., & Hansot, E. (1982). *Managers of virtue: Public school leadership in America, 1820–1980.* New York: Basic Books.

Urban, W. J. (1982). *Why teachers organized.* Detroit: Wayne State University Press.

Van de Kragt, A., Dawes, R., & Orbell, J. (1988). Are people who cooperate "rational altruists"? *Public Choice, 56,* 233–247.

Van Maanen, J., & Barley, S. R. (1984). Occupational communities: Culture and control in organizations. *Research in Organizational Behavior, 6,* 287–365.

Williams, R. C. (1979). The impact of collective bargaining on the principal: What do we know? *Education and Urban Society, 11*(2), 168–180.

Yamagishi, T. (1984). Development of distribution rules in small groups. *Journal of Personality and Social Psychology, 46,* 1069–1078.

Index

About the Author

Nina Bascia is Assistant Professor on the Faculty of Education at the University of Toronto. Her work and research interests include teacher leadership, the policies and practices that shape teachers' work, and teachers' formal and informal sources of professional development and identity. She works with organizations that support teacher-directed and -oriented educational change efforts in Canada and the United States. She is co-editor of *The Contexts of Teaching in Secondary Schools* (Teachers College Press, 1990, with Milbrey W. McLaughlin and Joan E. Talbert).